FROM EVERY STAGE

FROM EVERY STAGE

IMAGES OF AMERICA'S
ROOTS MUSIC

STEPHANIE P. LEDGIN

WITH A FOREWORD BY CHARLES OSGOOD

UNIVERSITY PRESS OF MISSISSIPPI / JACKSON

Publication of this book was supported
in part by a grant from Rebel Records.

www.upress.state.ms.us

Designed by Todd Lape

The University Press of Mississippi is a member of the
Association of American University Presses.

Library of Congress Cataloging-in-Publication Data

Ledgin, Stephanie P.
 From every stage : images of America's roots music /
Stephanie P. Ledgin ; with a foreword by Charles Osgood.—
1st ed.
  p. cm.
 Includes index.
 ISBN 1-57806-740-5 (cloth : alk. paper)
 1. Popular music—United States—Pictorial works. 2.
Musicians—United States—Interviews. 3. Bluegrass music—
Pictorial works. 4. Bluegrass musicians—Pictorial works. I.
Title.
 ML3477.L42 2005
 781.64'0973'022—dc22   2004023689

British Library Cataloging-in-Publication Data available

FOR TED,
THE BEST MUSIC IN MY LIFE

CONTENTS

FOREWORD

On the surface it would seem that photography and music are two very distinct and different art forms. One is for the eye, the other for the ear. One is suspended in space, the other in time. But true art in any form has the power to transform. These musicians and their instruments have the power to make wonderful pictures in the mind and heart. And this photographer with her instrument, the camera, has the power to evoke feelings, hopes, dreams, and memories. A photograph, like a song, can lift the spirit and touch the soul. Both can teach us something about ourselves.

Stephanie Ledgin calls this collection of hers "a photo narrative." And indeed it tells a story. Notice the instruments in these pictures. Each is perfect in its own way—its size, shape, texture, and design a perfect example of form following function. It must look a certain way to sound a certain way. It must sound a certain way to express a certain truth.

Notice the posture of the performers, the way they stand, the way they hold themselves when singing or dancing, and how they hold their instruments, blowing air through some, striking, picking, or strumming others. The musicians' bodies are instruments too, in the sense in which St. Francis used that word in his great prayer, "Lord, make me an instrument of Your peace."

Look especially at the faces in Ms. Ledgin's pictures. See the concentration there, the joy and radiance as the musicians focus on the sound and feel the beat. In life as in music, they say, timing is everything. That's also true in photography, where you must sense precisely the instant to click that shutter, to capture the light at a moment of truth. Turn these pages and you will not only see what I mean, you will feel and hear it too.

—CHARLES OSGOOD / JUNE 2004

PREFACE

Music, photographs, and a typewriter are among my earliest memories. It seems only natural that they come together here in these pages. My dad is a writer, originally a newspaper reporter-editor. I can still see him in my mind's eye sitting behind his desk, typing on his black manual typewriter, this when I was but a toddler of two or three.

Back then, the *Howdy Doody* theme song was my anthem, alternating with Mickey and Donald leading the *Club*, both of which were later replaced by "Happy Trails" whenever Roy and Dale would ride off at the conclusion of another successful TV episode. Beyond that, I was seemingly always surrounded by music from the get-go. All kinds of music. Broadway show tunes, standard folk songs popular in the fifties, music of the "great composers," and more. My mother is a classical pianist and violist; my father plays a variety of piano styles, sings, and "hoofs" a little. His dad, my grandpa Ledgin, was a tap dancer in vaudeville, and his mother, whom I never had the opportunity to know, played banjo and danced.

Photographs of my family were always very important to me. Someone in the family, be it at celebrations, on vacations, or just hanging out, had a still or movie camera in hand. Photographs served as and continue to be connections to my past, present, and future, through the eyes of so many relatives and friends, here and gone. In the mid-eighties, photos surfaced that I do not recall viewing previously of the grandmother I mentioned above. There

she was . . . with *my* face, *my* profile, *my* legs! I subsequently learned that, originally from what is now Austria, she had played folk style banjo in the early part of the twentieth century on New York area radio. What "folk style" referred to precisely, unfortunately I may never know.

The connection to my past took on an odd twist. In 1975, long before I had seen the photographs or knew about my grandmother having played banjo, I stumbled into bluegrass music as a professional journalist when I landed my first full-time editing position. Ending up with a career in folk and bluegrass music, albeit as a writer and photographer, was purely coincidental to my having answered a classified ad for an editorial job with a music magazine. In addition, while I knew music was in my genes, here before me, years later, were photographs of a family member directly involved in folk music.

In the mid-fifties, my family moved from New Jersey to Cajun country—Lake Charles, Louisiana. It's there that my musical memories kick in a little stronger. Such songs as "Jamaica Farewell" and "Banana Boat Song" sung by Harry Belafonte or "The Battle of New Orleans" from Johnny Horton come to mind. Naturally, it was also where strains of Cajun and zydeco music filtered into my life a bit. It was while living in the South that my folks gave me my first camera, a Kodak Tourist II, when I was about eight or nine years old.

During my formative years, my objectives in life were to be a Broadway dancer or an air force nurse. Then at sixteen, I took my first overseas trip and met people from a number of different cultures, speaking numerous languages. It was then I realized that I preferred the journalist's challenge of documenting life.

Most of my experience had been in investigative reporting and features writing, focusing on the popular music of my teens, sixties British and American rock, pop, and folk-rock. My family had provided impetus for a keen interest in a broad spectrum of folk genres, ranging from the politically correct sensibilities of folk portrayed by everyone from Paul Robeson and Woody Guthrie to Pete Seeger and Harry Belafonte, to ragtime and Yiddish music. And classical as well—my siblings and I were dragged to philharmonic concerts and I was subjected to piano lessons that never quite took for me. As a three-year-old, I began acrobatic and ballet lessons. There was a short stint in tap dancing class, but it was my paternal grandfather two decades later who gave me the basic time step that put me on the road to learning how to clog dance.

Fall of 1970, my first semester in college, brings my first vivid recollections of what I would later identify as bluegrass and other blended versions of it. It was the Nitty Gritty Dirt Band's *Uncle Charlie and His Dog Teddy* album, emanating from then-in-vogue supersized speakers blasting from the boys' dorm across the way. Within the next two years, I found myself attending two NGDB concerts where the sounds of fiddle and banjo filled my ears and started me on the road to expanding my musical tastes. A parting shot for me as I prepared to transfer to a school on the East Coast was an Elton John concert for which the Dillards were the opening act. They were the "Darling Family" on the old *Andy Griffith Show.* Talk about an interesting mix of music!

It was by pure chance that I ended up working professionally in bluegrass music and eventually in a variety of traditional folk genres. I answered a classified ad in the local paper for a writer-editor for a bluegrass publication, *Pickin'* magazine.

While my professional life in acoustic music started out in bluegrass, it has taken several routes and detours since that time, touching upon many genres of the broad folk music spectrum. I have worked in a variety of capacities that involved my journalism skills either directly or peripherally, ranging from publicity and public relations projects to artist management, event production, and festival management. I have returned "home" in recent years to focus on writing and photography within the genres that continue to tickle my fancy. This photo narrative reflects the past three decades.

This book is about expression, conveying the emotion, the passion of the music portrayed in still photos that make it possible to hear via these images. Musicians, singers, and dancers are captured for a split second in time.

While there in the faces of many, expression is not always limited to a grimace, a smile, or a studied look. Posture speaks volumes whether an artist is midperformance or caught candidly offstage. Among other factors contributing to bringing to the ear the images on these pages are the settings or circumstances in which the musicians and dancers were photographed. For some, the clothing worn adds to the persona. Other photographs depict legends who hold special historical significance.

There are many well-known faces, yet this is not a picture book of "who's who" in the broad spectrum of folk, country, blues, and roots music; therefore, you might not always find someone you are looking for. However, your eyes and ears will be filled with the music projected from these pages.

Also about expression are the interviews, excerpts, and quotes from important personalities, many of whom are no longer alive. In their own words, too, hear the music associated with each.

ACKNOWLEDGMENTS

I would like to thank my parents, Barbara and Norman, for giving me my first camera. My mother's ever-present movie camera at all family functions and vacations was true inspiration. They also instilled in me a love of, if not a passion and *need* for, music in my life.

To the twenty-two individuals who purchased this book sight unseen long before it was a reality, my heartfelt gratitude for their patience and near-blind faith. The same goes to the half a dozen retailers who expressed interest in including it in their sales catalogs, again, before I had a publisher.

A most gracious Charles Osgood, long-time anchor of *The Osgood File* and *CBS News Sunday Morning,* was kind enough to agree to write the foreword for this relatively unknown photographer. I am profoundly humbled by his participation. Words cannot express my gratitude to Mr. Osgood as well as to his assistant, Karen Beckers, for her diligent facilitation.

My sincere appreciation is extended to my editor, Craig Gill, who went to great lengths to make this project work as originally proposed. He has a fabulous editorial, art, and marketing staff who have been just wonderful to work with.

I am especially grateful to Judith McCulloh, whose insight and input were invaluable. Thank you to Dave Freeman and Rebel Records for sponsorship support.

Author interviewing Doc Watson. Clearwater's Great Hudson River Revival, Valhalla, New York, June 20, 1992.
© r/iveryahn

Over the past few years, the many folks at Klein & Ulmes Color Lab, Middlesex, New Jersey, have provided top-notch quality services for my photo needs. I would like to recognize Alan Goldstein, Dana Benner, Carole Debord, Linda Lodato, and especially Brian Mohan.

Certainly there would be no book without all the artists who are pictured, as well as the promoters who permitted photography at their venues. In addition, I was privileged to conduct interviews with many personalities through the years and appreciate their time and candor.

My thanks to Mark Moss and Scott Atkinson for allowing me to exhibit a sample of *From Every Stage* at the *Sing Out!* table at events. Thanks to all who helped identify some of those pictured whose names were lost to time. Special thanks to Lola Asbury and Bob O'Neal for backstage assistance at the Ryman, to Suzanne working security in the photo pit at MerleFest, and to Ken Weber, my "folkie" FedEx station rep. I appreciate the feedback given by my former colleagues at Rutgers University who previewed my book.

Thanks to Bob Yahn for snapping the candid shot of Doc Watson and me and for permitting its use here.

Finally, without the help of my husband, Ted Toskos, *From Every Stage* never would have been realized. His enduring love and support continue to amaze me.

New Grass Revival. Left to right: Béla Fleck, John Cowan, Sam Bush, Pat Flynn. The Bottom Line, New York City, June 9, 1988.

IN THE BEGINNING . . .

While I always had an interest in various types of popular folk music and, at the very least, a bent for banjo and fiddle, it wasn't until I landed an editorship at *Pickin'* magazine that bluegrass became a full-time career. I had heard a taste of bluegrass and traditional music growing up in both the Deep South and in the heart of America, Kansas City, Missouri. But it was primarily my journalism expertise, rather than any specific knowledge of bluegrass, that brought me on board *Pickin'*. That was July 1975 and the magazine was a little over a year young, enjoying its status as a formidable competitor to the two other mainstays of the music at the time, *Muleskinner News* and *Bluegrass Unlimited*. *Pickin'* stood apart in that it was a groundbreaking entity in its balanced focus on instruments as well as players.

In August 1975 I got my first introduction to "real" bluegrass musicians; we all went to a concert at the arts center in Holmdel, New Jersey, with Lester Flatt and the Nashville Grass headlining. I have to admit I didn't know what to make of a sixteen-year-old Marty Stuart looking just as cool as a teen could look in his black suit, white hat, and

Wade Mainer.

cowboy boots. I was in my early twenties and it was my first time seeing such a young, prominent musician. I was soon to learn that Marty was not so much the exception but that "youth rules" in some respects among bluegrassers—it's family music, often handed down and around among family members and friends. I would soon meet other such precociously talented kids, Mark O'Connor most notably. Of course, getting introduced to Mr. Flatt was pretty cool, too. (I used to get a kick out of Buddy Ebsen doing a little buck-and-wing to the music of Flatt and Scruggs on *The Beverly Hillbillies*.)

Not quite a year later, the powers-that-be at *Pickin'* finally let me out on my own, sending me to represent the magazine in Nashville at the annual Fan Fair. A highlight of the week was the all-star bluegrass concert. It was my first time shaking hands with the man himself, Bill Monroe, the "Father of Bluegrass."

Hanging out backstage then, as well as the following June when I returned for Fan Fair, I got to meet and greet such artists and behind-the-scenes people as Chet Atkins, Merle Travis, Kitty Wells, Grandpa and Ramona Jones, Jim and Jesse McReynolds, the whole McLain Family clan, Wade Mainer, Wilma Lee and Stoney Cooper, Ralph Stanley, along with his bass player Jack Cooke and guitarist Keith Whitley, Rounder Records' cofounder Ken Irwin, Patsy Montana, songwriters Jimmie Skinner and Paul Craft, and even the editor of a Japanese bluegrass publication. Japan was, and still is, one of the largest markets outside the United States for this American homegrown genre.

I was introduced to the Grand Ole Opry's official "hostess," Mrs. Tex Ritter (John's mom), whom I later would find myself chatting with backstage when I lived in Nashville for a couple of years and visited the Opry often. I remember well how she beamed and proudly told me about her son's new television series, *Three's Company*. To me, she epitomized the "Southern lady" image. The list goes on as the week did each of those two years.

Having spent several years of my childhood in Louisiana, I was also excited to meet Governor Jimmie Davis during that first trip to Nashville. Hearing and singing "You Are My Sunshine" during my youth made this photo op (at right) quite a keepsake. To this day the song remains one of my favorites and I was pleased to hear it revived in the film *O Brother, Where Art Thou?*

Bluegrass music and the pictures on these first four pages were just a beginning. The many roads I have traveled in traditional music are sampled in the pages that follow.

A technical note for the curious: photos taken prior to 1980 were made with any available, sometimes borrowed, camera. In 1980 I became more serious about photography and purchased my first 35 mm. From 1980 until 1998, I used two fully manual Minoltas, the SR-T 200 and 202b. Since 1998, I have shot with an automatic, a Minolta Maxxum 500si Super. In late 2003, I added a midrange digital, a Minolta Dimage s414. Four images in this book were taken with the digital. Much of my collection was shot with existing light, often with "pushed" film, thereby preserving the actual feel of given performances. Flash photography can be very distracting for artists on stage (as well as for the audience). It is not permitted at many venues.

Top: Governor Jimmie Davis and the author (photographer unknown). Bottom: Rounder Records founding partner Ken Irwin with Stoney and Wilma Lee Cooper. Fan Fair, Nashville, Tennessee, June 1976.

Members of Roy Acuff's Smoky
Mountain Boys, Bashful Brother
Oswald on dobro, with Charlie Collins,
guitar. "Martin Guitar Night" at Randy
Wood's Old Time Picking Parlor,
Nashville, Tennessee, June 1977.

Bill Monroe and the Blue Grass Boys. In the frame with Monroe are Bob Black, banjo, Randy Davis, bass, Wayne Lewis, guitar. Out of view is fiddler Kenny Baker. The New Deal, Madison, Tennessee, June 10, 1976.

★ ★ ★

BILL MONROE

"I LOVE TO BE ON THE ROAD"

"Father of Bluegrass" Bill Monroe was an imposing, dashing figure on stage. Dressed in summer whites or, in winter, dark suits, he would project a look of elegant sophistication within a music setting that so many people insist on hearing only in the context of hillbilly stereotypes. It was well known that if he liked you, he was kind and generous, but if you got on Mr. Monroe's bad side, he could snub you, at the very least.

While living in Nashville in the late seventies, I had gone to work for the Monroe Talent Agency, hired, supposedly, for my public relations abilities and booking contacts back east. But after only three weeks I quit, not wanting just to answer phones and make coffee, which, as it turned out, was what I was expected to do more than anything else. Let's just say it didn't work out.

Regardless, Bill did not talk to me for several years after that. In 1983 I was asked to interview him for *Country Rhythm* magazine. But when Bill saw I was the interviewer, he turned off and would only provide brief, if not empty, responses to my questions. Needless to say when everything was said and done, there just was not enough there for a good feature article.

Without warning a couple of years later, while photographing Bill's set on stage at the Vernon Valley Bluegrass Festival in New Jersey, I was looking through my lens and saw Bill turn to me and say something. He repeated, "Wanna dance?" So I put down my

camera and walked to center stage to join Bill, where we danced . . . as we did on many more occasions after that. That apparently ended the hard feelings he had harbored for years. The last time I spoke with Bill before he died was in 1994 at the Turning Point in Piermont, New York, where I emceed his two sets.

Here are a few choice comments from that failed interview, conducted on Bill's tour bus parked outside the Bottom Line in New York City, September 2, 1983. They provide some glimpses into the mind of a much-beloved musician. His final comment was one fans would often hear him say; Bill Monroe thrived on that encouragement.

SL: *Was there anything else in your life you wanted to pursue as much or more than music?*
BM: No, music was it. It was just in me; I knew that I was goin' to do it.

SL: *At this point in your life, do you feel that you have achieved everything you ever really wanted to do musically?*
BM: Ah, there might be a couple of things that I would like to do, but I've got done most of them.

SL: *What keeps your music forever young?*

BM: Working hard at it, taking care of it, playing it the best you can play.

SL: *What other types of music do you listen to?*
BM: Some classical is all right, some rock and roll is all right. But a lot of it I don't like, where it's got too much noise in it and just a hard beat that ain't no music there. There's just a single word that they've got to sing. There's a lot of people that plays good music. I like western swing music. I like the old colored blues, music like that, the old-time fiddle music.

SL: *Do you ever plan on retiring?*
BM: No, I'm not planning on retiring.

SL: *Would you trade being on the road so much with any-thing else?*
BM: No, I love to be on the road.

SL: *What do you think about the growth in numbers of bluegrass festivals over the last decade?*
BM: Well, they're all over the country now . . . We just find festivals in every state now. And I like to be there with them.

SL: *We hope ten years from now you'll still be there!*
BM: If you help me I will.

—BILL MONROE / 1911–1996

In a familiar gesture, Monroe tips his hat as he hits the closing notes of a song. Lone Star Café, New York City, January 13, 1987.

Above: Bill Monroe picks near his record table, surrounded by admiring fans while the festival audience, visible in left field of photo, watches the stage show. In the white T-shirt is Karl Aasland, mandolinist for the Norwegian bluegrass band Gone At Last, also appearing at the event that day. Waterloo Bluegrass Festival, Waterloo Village, Stanhope, New Jersey, August 23, 1986.

Right: Grand finale jam. All eyes are on former Blue Grass Boy, fiddler Kenny Baker. New York City Bluegrass Festival, Snug Harbor Cultural Center, Staten Island, New York, June 30, 1985.

Snuffy Jenkins was a prominent North Carolina three-finger banjo stylist. It is this approach to playing banjo (versus two-finger technique) that fellow North Carolinian Earl Scruggs brought to Bill Monroe's Blue Grass Boys when he became a member of that group in 1945. "Scruggs style," Earl's energized three-finger playing, is what has come to be identified with bluegrass music.

Left: Snuffy Jenkins is caught during a candid moment backstage at Carnegie Hall. This photograph first appeared in *Masters of the 5-String Banjo* by Pete Wernick and Tony Trischka. Above: Snuffy Jenkins, Pappy Sherrill and the Hired Hands pose for a publicity shot on stage at Carnegie's Weill Recital Hall, New York City, November 17, 1984.

Earl Scruggs with fiddler Glen Duncan in background. Count Basie Theatre, Red Bank, New Jersey, October 24, 2002.

Above: Roland White. Bluegrass Fan
Fest, Galt House, Louisville, Kentucky,
October 4, 2003.

Left: David "Dawg" Grisman, innovative
jazz-grass mandolinist. The Bottom
Line, New York City, July 20, 1987.

★ ★ ★

AND WHEN IN NASHVILLE . . .
THE WORLD-FAMOUS STATION INN

Since 1974 when it first opened its doors, the Station Inn has been a "homeplace" for bluegrass pickers, drawing listeners from near and far. Today, more than thirty years later, it rightfully boasts of itself as "The World-Famous Station Inn."

Its stage has been graced by virtually everybody in bluegrass—Bill Monroe, John McEuen, Del McCoury, Peter Rowan, Ralph Stanley, Larry Sparks . . . The list of names goes clear around the world as it includes bands from other countries as well.

It is interesting to go back and listen to a couple of comments, recorded February 1, 1978, made by veteran Nashville songwriter-vocalist Billy Smith and the legendary Roland White (Kentucky Colonels, Nashville Bluegrass Band, and others). What they described then is just as apt now. The Station Inn's renown has endured and grown. It remains the place of choice for residents of and visitors to Music City.

BILLY SMITH: Sometimes this place will fill up with people where we know everybody.

ROLAND WHITE: Yes, and then there are times when it fills up that I don't know nearly any of them. Word's gotten around. Everywhere I go, the country people ask me, "What do you do when you're in Nashville?" I say, "I play the Station Inn." A lot of other people talk about the Station Inn. And a lot of people come in from out of town that don't know a thing about bluegrass, yet they head for the Station Inn. That's the truth. I see people from everywhere, the Netherlands, Australia, England, all over the United States, in here all the time.

BILLY: What draws people here is the atmosphere. [The people that come] are supportive, real supporters of the music. The audience is very supportive. They know what good music is.

Above: The Seldom Scene's John Duffey (Mike Auldridge in background). Waterloo Bluegrass Festival, Waterloo Village, Stanhope, New Jersey, August 24, 1985.

Right: Nashville Bluegrass Band's Mike Compton, with Mark Hembree on bass. In background obscured, Stuart Duncan playing fiddle, Pat Enright, guitar, Alan O'Bryant, banjo. Winterhawk (now Grey Fox) Bluegrass Festival, Ancramdale, New York, July 1987.

Jay Ungar and daughter Ruth Ungar, appearing with Jay and wife Molly Mason's group, Swingology. Jay is the composer of "Ashokan Farewell," popularized as the recurring theme in Ken Burns's epic PBS series *The Civil War*. Ruth also performs in the Mammals, "subversive acoustic traditionalists," along with Pete Seeger's grandson, Tao Rodriguez-Seeger. Philadelphia Folk Festival, Schwenksville, Pennsylvania, August 25, 2001.

Above: Ed Ferris, while bass player with Bill Harrell and the Virginians. New York City Bluegrass Festival, Snug Harbor Cultural Center, Staten Island, New York, June 24, 1984.

Left: Art Stamper. Fiddler for such notable bluegrass acts as the Stanley Brothers, the Osborne Brothers, and the Goins Brothers. World of Bluegrass, Galt House, Louisville, Kentucky, September 29, 2003.

Scottish fiddler Johnny Cunningham, pictured during his days as a member of Silly Wizard. I was kneeling in the aisle a few rows from the stage, attempting to snap a shot while John was doing a solo set. He saw me just below the spotlights and said something to the effect of "will you take the damn photo already?" but in a good-natured way. At that, he stopped playing for a split second as I grabbed this shot. Triplex Theater, Borough of Manhattan Community College, New York City, June 1, 1985.

Lynn Morris Band. Shown with Lynn are Jesse Brock on mandolin and Marshall Wilborn playing bass. Deer Path Park, Readington Township, New Jersey, June 28, 2001.

Above: Multi-instrumentalist, multi-genre performer David Bromberg. Philadelphia Folk Festival, Schwenksville, Pennsylvania, August 27, 1989.

Left: Folk singer and actor Josh White, Jr. Old Songs Festival of Traditional Music and Dance, Altamont, New York, June 26, 1999.

Folk and blues stylist Odetta. Note the swirls of smoke coming off the end of her guitar peghead where she has a stick of incense burning. On another occasion at Carnegie Hall, I was attending a live taping of Garrison Keillor's *A Prairie Home Companion*. As Garrison is known to do, he led the house in singing a song, possibly "Tell Me Why," but I do not recall. He had us all on our feet, out of our seats following his lead in verse after verse, making up humorous lyrics as he went. At one point, a powerful voice overtook all others around me and I turned to find that it was Odetta, standing directly behind me, tears of laughter streaming down her face even as she sang in her distinctive voice. I remember our eyes met and she smiled even wider, then laughed at being "caught in the act," and kept on singing. A Folk Celebration, Carnegie Hall, New York City, May 17, 1985.

Traditional Kentucky singer and mountain dulcimer artist Jean Ritchie. I met Jean
Ritchie during my first year with *Pickin'* magazine when I went to Port Washington,
New York, for a concert given by the McLain Family Band, who were friends of hers
from Kentucky. The elegant simplicity of her renditions of old ballads epitomizes her
performances; Jean's repertoire draws from oral tradition as well as from her fine
songwriting. It was a highlight of my own career and very special to me when she
agreed to headline at the 1998 New Jersey Folk Festival, where I was then director.
A Folk Celebration, Carnegie Hall, New York City, May 17, 1985.

Country and bluegrass star Ricky Skaggs (right) jams Cajun style with Christine Balfa (above) and Balfa Toujours. Dirk Powell is playing accordion, pictured to Ricky's right. Delaware Valley Bluegrass Festival, Woodstown, New Jersey, September 2, 2000.

Above: The Happy (left) and Artie Traum Band with bassist Roly Salley (on Happy's right and partially obscured). Roly became a member of the Chris Isaak Band in 1985. Right: The Happy Traum Band with (left to right) Happy, Roly, and multi-instrumentalist Larry Campbell. Larry has worked with a who's who of artists in a wide range of genres. He joined Bob Dylan's band in 1997. He continues to record with and produce albums for a diverse number of artists. The Traums were an integral part of the burgeoning sixties "rootsy" folk scene in the New York area, performing with such artists as Dylan, the Band and Paul Butterfield. Artie continues to tour extensively, while Happy and his wife Jane oversee Homespun Tapes, which they founded nearly four decades ago. Both shots were taken at the legendary Greenwich Village club Gerdes Folk City, New York City, (top) August 7, 1983, (bottom) December 9, 1983.

Left: Janette Carter plays autoharp in the tradition of her mother and aunt while brother Joe Carter accompanies her on guitar. They are the children of early country music pioneers A. P. and Sara Carter. "Mother" Maybelle Carter was their aunt. They continue to keep traditional mountain music alive by maintaining the Carter Family Fold in Hiltons, Virginia, where they present artists in concert. McLain Family Festival, Big Hill Farm near Berea, Kentucky, August 15, 1982.

Above: Three important figures in the history of the development of bluegrass: (from left) Don Stover, Red Rector, and Bill Clifton. Stover was prominent on the Boston bluegrass scene, while Clifton carried the music across oceans to other continents. Rector served as a transitional figure between early players of bluegrass mandolin and the more relaxed "second generation" of pickers. Waterloo Bluegrass Festival, Waterloo Village, Stanhope, New Jersey, August 23, 1980.

Playing bodhran, Phil Smillie of the
Tannahill Weavers from Scotland.
The Bottom Line, New York City,
September 19, 1984.

Above: *The Masters of the Folk Violin* was a concept tour created by the National Council for the Traditional Arts. Six fiddlers representing a variety of genres demonstrated their styles separately and together. Featured during its earliest concert dates were the teenaged Alison Krauss (western long bow), bluegrass master fiddler Kenny Baker with support from legendary dobro man Josh Graves, Cajun fiddler Michael Doucet of Beausoleil accompanied by brother David on guitar, Kansas City jazzman Claude Williams with accompanist John Stewart, Irish style from Seamus Connolly and Joe Cormier performing music of Cape Breton with Barbara MacDonald Magone backing him on piano. Pictured are fiddlers Williams and Krauss. This was the first major concert I produced. As a photojournalist, I have often found it challenging when managing an event to take time to handle a camera as well. A thousand people showed up for this unprecedented presentation. Julia Richman High School Auditorium, New York City, March 5, 1988.

Right: Award-winning bluegrass songwriter Lynn Morris. Deer Path Park, Readington Township, New Jersey, June 28, 2001.

Singer-songwriter Shawn Colvin.
Shawn appeared on this occasion as
a guest artist with banjo player Akira
Satake's eclectic bluegrass band,
which was the opening act for Eddie
Adcock and Talk of the Town, part of
the Sunday bluegrass series I produced at the Lone Star Café. The
night before, Colvin had won a New
York Music Award. A year later she
took home a Grammy. Lone Star Café,
New York City, April 10, 1988.

Above: Warming up in the green room: Jim Hurst (guitar), Missy Raines (bass), Mark Schatz (banjo), Casey Driessen (fiddle). Bluegrass Fan Fest, Galt House, Louisville, Kentucky, October 2002.

Right: Banjo legend J. D. Crowe. Bluegrass Fan Fest, Galt House, Louisville, Kentucky, October 4, 2003.

Pat Cannon calls the squares for her Foot and Fiddle Dance Company, stepping lively to the music of Mindy J. and the Cyclone Rangers. Grand Old Country Music Show, Lyndhurst, Tarrytown, New York, August 7, 1982.

Left: Songwriter and country star Jim Lauderdale has participated in recent years in several bluegrass projects with Ralph Stanley. In this photo, he had joined Patty Loveless on stage. MerleFest, Wilkesboro, North Carolina, May 1, 2004.

Above: Ralph Stanley leads the Clinch Mountain Boys in singing "Angel Band." Delaware Valley Bluegrass Festival, Woodstown, New Jersey, September 1, 2001.

Utah Phillips, "left of center" activist singer-songwriter. Philadelphia Folk Festival, Schwenksville, Pennsylvania, August 25, 2001.

JENS KRÜGER
CATCHES THE "FEEL"

The Krüger Brothers from Switzerland are something of a phenomenon in bluegrass music circles. Brothers Jens, banjo, and Uwe, guitar, having performed together professionally since 1973, teamed up nearly two decades later with American transplant Joel Landsberg on bass. The Krügers each pursued other musical interests individually along the way but eventually settled in as the Appalachian Barn Orchestra, whose sound is faithfully reflected in their current-day programs.

They wowed the crowds not only in Europe but in the original "land of bluegrass," winning the hearts of American fans. So popular have they become that, in 2003, they moved their families to the hills of North Carolina, their home base from which they continue to tour extensively.

In 1985, on vacation in Switzerland, I met up with Jens while he was a member of The Bluegrass Family, an ensemble of pickers living together communally on a farm where they were honing their bluegrass skills. The Bluegrass Family was about to embark on its inaugural annual festival, which the group hosts each August near Zurich. After I interviewed the group, they picked up their instruments and played an hour's worth of music for an audience of one under the trees on their farm.

Jens played with the group for about four years, learning everything bluegrass he could lay his fingers and ears on. Then a nearly twenty-three-year-old newlywed, he was already demonstrating extreme prowess on the banjo.

"I sang a lot as a kid with my mother, who was a kindergarten teacher. I played harmonica at age five. Dad was in the States in the fifties. He got lots of records of country and hillbilly.

"At eleven, I started to play banjo, tenor banjo. I didn't know the difference. I played Dixieland for five years and at sixteen found I had the wrong banjo for bluegrass. So my brother bought a twenty-five-dollar frailing banjo. I've played it since then.

"Earl Scruggs is my main influence. I took jazz tunes on tenor and transposed them to the five-string. Don Reno, John Hickman, Bill Emerson, J. D. Crowe. They have the feel even if they play it ten different ways. I try to catch the feel. That to me is the most important part of the music."

—JENS KRÜGER
STETTEN, SWITZERLAND, AUGUST 2, 1985

Jens Krüger, Stetten, Switzerland,
August 2, 1985.

Above: Tex-Mex conjunto accordionist Flaco Jiménez.
Lone Star Café, New York City, March 27, 1985.

Left: Ex-Byrd Chris Hillman, heading up the Desert Rose
Band, which he co-founded with John Jorgenson. The
Bottom Line, New York City, August 13, 1987.

Above: Flying hands with Walt Michael and Company. Michael (left) duels with John Kirk on the hammered dulcimer for a speedy rendition of "Golden Slippers," while bassist Mark Murphy's hands can be seen playing hard to keep up on bass. Peaceful Valley Bluegrass Festival, Shinhopple, New York, July 12, 1986.

Right: Doyle Lawson looking toward camera, with Quicksilver band member Jamie Dailey on guitar. Delaware Valley Bluegrass Festival, Woodstown, New Jersey, August 30, 2003.

Above: Country and bluegrass singer Rose Maddox belts one out, backed by members of Kentucky Roots: Randy Bailey playing upright, Bob Harris on guitar, and Steve Lutke on banjo. Peaceful Valley Bluegrass Festival, Shinhopple, New York, July 12, 1986.

Right: Tom Rowe of Schooner Fare. The Bottom Line, New York City, October 11, 1987.

Above: Amy Fradon (left) and Leslie Ritter, appearing with the Artie Traum Band. The Bottom Line, New York City, April 28, 1987.

Right: Karl Aasland of Gone At Last, a bluegrass group from Norway. Lone Star Café, New York City, August 29, 1986.

Above: Dudley Connell of the Johnson Mountain Boys. David McLaughlin on mandolin and Marshall Wilborn on bass. Delaware Bluegrass Festival, Gloryland Park, Glasgow, Delaware, September 6, 1987.

Left: Pat Cannon's Foot and Fiddle Dance Company (left to right): Germaine Goodson, Margaret Morrison, Pat Cannon, Debbie Thomas. Queens Bluegrass Festival, Queens Farm, Floral Park, Queens, New York, August 15, 1987.

Above: Dry Branch Fire Squad's Suzanne Thomas. Philadelphia Bluegrass Festival, Plymouth–White Marsh High School, Plymouth Meeting, Pennsylvania, March 9, 1990.

Right: Raymond W. McLain, while touring with Jim (in background) and Jesse and the Virginia Boys. Delaware Valley Bluegrass Festival, Woodstown, New Jersey, September 5, 1992.

BEAUSOLEIL AVEC MICHAEL DOUCET

MASH-DOWN MUSIC

After three decades of recording and touring internationally, Beausoleil *avec* Michael Doucet remains the foremost Cajun music ensemble. Beausoleil performances are about as high energy as it gets, with dancing to the music a must.

When I first heard them in 1982 at the Smithsonian's Festival of American Folklife in Washington, D.C., they had just begun to take this country by storm, having experienced success first in such French-speaking countries as Canada and France and in other parts of Europe, then filtering into the American patchwork via folk festivals. In New York City in the mid-eighties for a number of performances, including some with Canray Fontenot, the great Creole fiddler, Doucet took a few minutes after one of those concerts to offer some thoughts on Cajun music. He emphasized that the Acadian heritage is long and deep in southwest Louisiana. The music of the region was first recorded around 1929–1931 as "race" records, and those recordings "probably encompass eighty percent of what you call Acadian repertoire, Cajun repertoire today." Here are some of his timeless comments taped March 15, 1986, Washington Square Church, New York City.

SL: *Cajun music is a living tradition. Do you feel you are innovators within this tradition?*

MD: Definitely, because we live in the eighties and I'm totally against somebody being a clone, imitating someone who came before him. Appreciating and imitating are two different things. I'm fortunate, lucky enough to have studied with some of the great musicians like Dennis McGee, Canray Fontenot, the Balfa Brothers, and different people like that. What I've done and what they've always impressed upon me was to develop my own style. And you do have your own style; it's where you come from. But the fact is it's learning the songs correctly and learning the nuances, because nobody can explain it to you. Nobody can ever really explain to me what goes where.

There are some people who are curious; there are some who aren't. I've always enjoyed creating things, writing songs, playing improvisational music. And within the structure, it's very improvisational, but you have to have the structure. It is completely nothing if the structure is not solid.

SL: *With all the energy you expend each night in concert, how do you make each performance "new and exciting" not only for the audience but for yourselves?*
MD: It's mostly just the contact with the people. You can tell right off where they're from, what they expect, if they expect a rock and

roll band, an old band or whatever. We're just us. That's what they get. We don't play wimpy music. We play mash-down music. The minute we start, it's a locomotive, you know. If you want to get on board, it's there.

We play this music because we really care and because we're really scared what could happen to it commercially. As strong as we want to be with traditional, we take a laid-back approach, because that's the way we've always done things. It's not a flash in the pan. We're going to be playing the music when we're seventy years old.

Above: Errol Verret played accordion with Beausoleil for ten years. He is a highly skilled maker of the instrument, crafting his Evangeline accordions. The Bottom Line, New York City, August 29, 1986.

Left: Creole fiddler Canray Fontenot flanked by Beausoleil's fiddler Michael Doucet and guitarist David Doucet. Carnegie Hall's Weill Recital Hall, New York City, April 21, 1985.

Above: Bill Keith. A view from the balcony. Lone Star Café, New York City, July 26, 1984.

Right: Bill Monroe and the Blue Grass Boys. Long-time sideman Kenny Baker is on fiddle in the foreground, his posture in profile readily recognizable. The Bottom Line, New York City, September 2, 1983.

Above: Pete Seeger (left) and Jug Band leader Jim Kweskin.
Clearwater's Great Hudson River Revival, Croton Point Park,
Croton-on-Hudson, New York, June 21, 1986.

Left: Mr. Spoons. New York City Bluegrass Festival, Snug Harbor
Cultural Center, Staten Island, New York, July 17, 1983.

Multi-instrumental bluegrass talent Jimmy Arnold (above) teams up with dobro stylist Stacy Phillips (right). The Bottom Line, New York City, January 11, 1986.

Richie Havens. "Freedom" became an anthem for the Woodstock generation. Lincoln Center Out-of-Doors Festival, Damrosch Park, New York City, August 24, 1986.

Above: Phil Smillie of the Tannahill Weavers. Phil is one of the two remaining original members, along with Roy Gullane. The Bottom Line, New York City, September 19, 1984.

Right: Merle Watson. Son of legendary guitarist Doc Watson, Merle went on the road with his father within months of first picking up a guitar to learn to play. Waterloo Folk Festival, Waterloo Village, Stanhope, New Jersey, September 3, 1984.

Above: Jonathan Edwards, folk-pop songwriter-vocalist.
The Bottom Line, New York City, October 11, 1987.

Right: Frank Vignola, with Mark O'Connor's Hot Swing
Trio. MerleFest, Wilkesboro, North Carolina, April 30, 2004.

ROY M. HUSKEY
IN HIS OWN WORDS

Roy M. Huskey, like his father, "Junior" Huskey (Roy M. Huskey, Jr.), was a bass player's bass player. The senior Huskey played on a plethora of country artist classics, including the legendary initial *Will the Circle Be Unbroken* recording and the Byrds' bluegrass-and-country tinged *Sweetheart of the Rodeo*. Both musicians were ace Nashville session men, much in demand, the younger having followed in his father's footsteps upon "Junior" Huskey's death from cancer at age forty-three.

The son's playing can be heard on hundreds, if not thousands, of albums. In addition to his extensive studio work, he toured with such performers as Emmylou Harris, the O'Kanes, John Hartford, Steve Earle, T Bone Burnett and Peter Rowan, to name a few. And he appeared on volume II of the *Circle* series. Technically and legally, "Jr." was not a part of his name; his father was already Huskey, Jr., and father and son had different middle names. But he was fondly referred to by friends as "Roy, Jr." Sadly, he passed away at age forty, also from cancer.

Roy M. Huskey. The Bottom Line, New York City, November 17, 1985.

I first met Roy, Jr., while he was on tour with Peter Rowan in 1985. We sat down later that year, before a gig he was working with John Hartford, to tape an in-depth interview for a tentative feature. Roy was candid, forthcoming, modest, warm, and witty, with a decidedly offbeat but endearing sense of humor. His asides were colorful and priceless. Years later, after he had died, his wife, Lisa, told me that Roy rarely gave interviews and that she knew of only one other that had gone to print.

This conversation took place at The Turning Point, Piermont, New York, November 24, 1985. It appears here almost in its entirety, save for nonrelevant chatter. Questions have been shortened, but Roy's responses are essentially verbatim, as his historic biography seems best told by Roy himself.

SL: *Was your father the biggest influence on you in your deciding to play bass?*
RH: Probably so, I really couldn't say, to be honest with you. I've had a lot of influences, a lot!

SL: *Do you have some thoughts or memories you'd like to share about your dad?*

RH: I can tell you this . . . he was gone all the time, working sessions. On weekends he was mostly at home. We had a lake we used to go fishing at, and some stuff like that. And we'd take trips sometimes back to east Tennessee to see some folks and all of that kind of thing. That's such a broad question; you've got me.

SL: *Did your dad teach you bass, or how did you learn?*

RH: I started playing it by learning along with the records, that type of thing, mainly.

SL: *Because your dad played bass?*

RH: It was about the only thing I could really figure anything out on at that time.

SL: *How old were you?*

RH: Twelve years old.

SL: *Any professional training, or are you solely self-taught?*

RH: Yeah, I've had a small amount of professional training, maybe close to a year's worth. And I've had some piano training, too, a couple of years of that.

SL: *So you read music?*

RH: Right, but not real fluently, though.

SL: *Was it classical training or strictly country or bluegrass?*

RH: Classical, all of it.

SL: *Do you play other instruments in addition to bass and piano?*

RH: Now wait, let me clarify that. I don't *play* piano. I play "at" it. I've tried to play just about anything I could get my hands on, some mandolin, some guitar, some bass, of course piano. And yes, at one time I did do some work on piano, some sessions. Only easy things *(laughing)*. I've also learned a little bit of fiddle. Now don't put that in there. Somebody might ask me about it and I'll regret it! Say I played "at" them or played "with" them.

SL: *How and when did your professional career begin?*

RH: September, no, October of 1971, very shortly after my dad died, I started working.

SL: *How did it come about? What did you do?*

RH: I called a lot of people trying to get some type of work or something going. One of the first ones I called who was interested was Del Wood. And Del said she might be able to get me a spot playing behind her on the Opry. I guess in that way I was pretty lucky. I had been working for some time before that, too. Some rock and roll garage bands and such and some high school things.

SL: *You debuted (professionally) on the Opry?*

RH: At least as far as being in the union and all that is concerned. I played a lot of other things, too, before. The Opry, that's where the upright bass work came in. All the other stuff was rock and roll with electric bass.

SL: *With your working on the Opry, do you feel that you are playing in the shadows, or perhaps through the shadows, of the notoriety of your dad?*

RH: Oh yeah! But it doesn't really seem to present any particular obstacle. My worst typecasting that may occur occurs due to my own career, really. People typecast me as strictly bluegrass which I'm not strictly a bluegrass player. I may play a little, if anything. But that's kind of where I started out, though, is in the bluegrass field. That's what I started listening to [and] practicing and stuff like that.

SL: *Who were your earliest influences?*

RH: Well, I could name two right off the bat which would be Bill Monroe and Lester Flatt.

SL: *Their bass players at the time or their music in general?*
RH: Mostly just the music in general.

SL: *Other than your dad, has there been any other bass player whom you tried to emulate or whose style you tried to follow?*
RH: Any of them that played a lick that I liked! You want some names on that? Bob Moore was one. I picked up some style from Billy Linneman, 'cause we worked together a lot. He was a staff player at the Opry. Henry Strezlecki, of course, was very influential. I also had a certain amount of jazz influence later from some other bass players, some who I'm not even sure of the names, since the names weren't always printed on the albums. If I taped off the radio, I wouldn't know who it was. I just picked it up and heard it.

SL: *Are you as good a bass player as your dad?*
RH: No, definitely not. I'm working on it. And you know, there's no way, even if I ever did get, so to speak, that good, you can't copy a style. I wish I could. You can only go so far.

SL: *Can you describe your style; is it unique?*
RH: Oh, boy, my style is very haphazard, and as far as being unique, yes, certain parts of it are very much my own. Because my dad wasn't able to teach me a lot—I heard a lot of his work. But he worked so much that he didn't have any time to teach me. I had to pick it up mostly on my own from watching what few others I got to watch.

SL: *Did you do any picking at home with your dad or with other family members?*
RH: No, very little. I wish we had.

SL: *You never played an actual gig with your dad?*
RH: No.

SL: *Tell me more about your family. Is your mother musical?*
RH: Yes, quite so. Her family had a band. And they used to work out of Sparta, Tennessee. You heard that, Benny? *(Speaking aside to no one.)* Benny Martin. He's from Sparta. He used to pick with us. My dad was picking with him since the time he was a kid. That's of course how he and my mom got together. Her dad was a pop fiddler and everybody in the family did pick something and they all sang. I don't have any recordings from them or anything.

SL: *Do you have brothers and sisters?*
RH: I've got a brother and he plays the radio and he plays the "bango" [banjo]. He just started on that about three months ago. He ain't doing too bad for the length of time. He had studied a little piano, but he never really had the interest to keep it going. Mechanically, for classical and such, he probably would have been excellent. He picked up very fast.

SL: *Where were you born and raised?*
RH: Where was I born and raised? I was born and raised at *(gives his street address)* in Nashville, Tennessee. I'm twenty-nine and I'm still living right there. I've never moved from there *(laughs)*. This is going to be a strange interview *(spoken solemnly)*.

SL: *How many basses do you own?*
RH: At this point, I have six and all of them except for one are plywood. And three of the plywoods seem to have an extraordinary tone to them, at least for recording. Two Gretsches and an American Standard. But I've known people to have good luck with about anything, if it's set up right. I do own one straight wood bass, an old German bass, about 1920. Right now it's setting at home with no strings on it. I'm going to be fixing it up soon, hopefully.

SL: *What kind of strings do you prefer?*
RH: It depends on what I'm going to use it for. But what I usually use in this field [bluegrass], I use gut strings. La Bella. I'm giving

them advertisement. Incidentally, their "A" string's winding [is] the one that comes unwound a lot.

SL: *What do you carry on the road?*
RH: I have a Kay that's about, I figure somewhere around a 1940, maybe late thirties bass. It was my dad's first bass that somehow or another, through Don Gibson who had it, it wound up coming back to me. I'm using that one, as a matter of fact, on this deal. It's been on a lot of stuff itself, a lot of the Carl Smith stuff, and things my dad did, some of the early Flatt and Scruggs stuff. John [Hartford] finds a fascination with the fact that it's on a lot of the Lester and Earl tapes he's got.

It's got a sticker on it from Sho-Bud, but Sho-Bud is in Madison, Tennessee, rather than Nashville. When they first started it, it was in a little shack, maybe about the size of this room, maybe about two foot from the railroad tracks. I also could relate some stories on that, but none that could be printed!

How about my dad's ooga horn? It got lost out there. We had an ooga horn we had on an old '59 Pontiac. We bought a Tempest in '62 when they came out. We were going to have the ooga horn put on the Tempest. The shop was going to wire it up for us and I don't know if someone stole the ooga horn or it got lost out there or what. It [Sho-Bud] was right on the edge of Madison out toward Hendersonville. The shack is gone; it has been for many years.

SL: *Who do you listen to in current music for ideas?*
RH: Well, for one, my radio's broke, so I don't get to listen to a lot. Well, any car I own, the radio is dead, completely dead, AM or FM. We do listen some at home. My wife loves rock and roll, so we do listen to a lot of that. I listen sometimes to WSM in the nighttime.

But most of the time, any innovation I do usually is done on the job. Maybe it's something that's entered my mind and I'll try this little idea I got while sitting in the [living room] chair one day. It tends to work sometimes; sometimes it don't. But I try all kinds of things.

You know, music hasn't really changed, at least I don't think, much in my field. Music hasn't changed much since disco. They took the electric bass about as outrageous as it can go. Nonetheless, though, it's just something that kind of happens when it happens. Plus I experiment a lot when I play live. That amounts to a lot. A lot of stuff I can use later in the studios.

SL: *The audience primes you?*
RH: Oh, yes, definitely, and so do the other players, the artists. Anything can inspire me into any idea at any time if I've got an instrument in my hands.

SL: *Have you been a band member with anyone or have you always been freelance?*
RH: I've just about always been freelance.

SL: *Name some you've worked with.*
RH: Now you're asking me names! *(Laughing.)* Okay, well, I've never really done much touring. Most of my work has been local. I've done a little bit here and there. As of yet, I've never actually went out around the country to play. That'll look real good in a magazine. But I have worked with quite a few people over the years. I should have brought a list!

I've worked some, off and on, it's also hard to explain, some of the conditions I've worked under. Like I worked for Bill for a while, Bill Monroe, but that was under a nightclub, which they weren't paying union wages. He wouldn't allow his band to work there, but I went ahead and worked there until I figured the union would close in. I've worked, of course, with John [Hartford], Benny Martin. I've worked some for Roy Acuff, Jim and Jesse, Peter Rowan. I'm naming mainly people in the bluegrass field. On the Opry I've worked behind just about everybody there.

SL: *What about festivals, local gigs, Station Inn?*

RH: Not a whole lot. Most of my bluegrass stuff has been done in the studio. One reason people do call me is the fact that I'm a local player. If they do need a bass player, maybe their bass player quit, they can get hold of me quick, 'cause I'm usually in town. I worked some with Jimmy Martin in the studio.

SL: *Any memorable Opry dates?*
RH: A lot has happened over the years. I'm sure there have been, but you've caught me at a time when my mind is blank.

SL: *Has there been one artist, anybody that stands out in your mind, that was exceptionally comfortable to work with?*
RH: Just about everybody.

SL: *You are currently working the Opry regularly. Are you part of the official Opry band?*
RH: I'm really a substitute for a staff player. They don't consider me on the staff, but a lot of people do consider me on the staff, so I don't really know what my status is at this point. I just show up when the other bass player ain't there and they need somebody to work.

SL: *Are you more comfortable in the studio or on stage?*
RH: It's just different. As long as I'm comfortable, I'm comfortable either way.

SL: *Have you ever had a bad gig?*
RH: Oh, yes, I don't think I'd better elaborate on that. Well, I could elaborate, just don't print it. You know, occasionally somebody'll just have a bad day. They need somebody to blame it on, why not the bass player? Everybody in Nashville knows I'll take just about anything. It's probably another reason I get called as much as I do.

SL: *You don't mean that in the "down and out" sense, right, about taking just anything?*

RH: Well, now I can't really say that because a lot of times I'll work for nothing trying to help people out. Maybe they want to cut a record and if it's someone I know, particularly someone that's been around in the business, like Clyde Moody or somebody. I've done a thing or two for him. But I think in one case he was able to pay me, in the other case I never heard anything about it. But you know, I don't mind doing that. Because it's just part of the business. They cut the record and . . . it's what's called cutting [on] spec. But it's illegal to do for the union. But a lot of people do it now. The union doesn't have the control it had fifteen or twenty years ago, 'cause we've got so many studios and they can't police everything. You can't police a hundred studios, which now we have well over a hundred. Twenty years ago we had five.

SL: *What is the most difficult task for you in the studio or on stage?*
RH: Getting there on time *(laughs)*. Definitely.

SL: *Any sessions that have left an imprint in your memory?*
RH: Yeah, I do have quite a few. Just about every session I consider is one, and very special at a time. And whenever I'm working for someone, that artist I try to give number-one [attention] to, always. It makes the artist feel better. It makes for better relations between me and them. It makes the session go better.

SL: *How much input do you have in sessions?*
RH: It varies. Some people give me a lot. And sometimes I just come and I'm expected to sit in the corner and shut up. So that varies from one extreme to the other.

SL: *Do you have specific goals or dreams in music?*
RH: Just to be able to get better at what I'm doing and to keep improving. I don't ever want to stagnate. I can't *stand* to stagnate, which I have at times and which, when I do, I get desperate to go out. But I'd like to get better at it. I don't particularly have anything at this time that I'm working on. But I have done a few other things

here and there. I do have a publishing company and a record label and I have been known to produce or coproduce things. But I'm not active really in that at this time.

SL: *Do you compose?*
RH: No, I wish I did. John Hartford's wanting to get me into that.

You're asking me these questions, and a lot of my answers I know are vague. But my career, due to the nature, a lot of things happened almost by luck, or maybe I just happened to be in the right club at the right time, to run into somebody and get to talking to them and a few weeks later I may get called for a session. But a lot of it almost didn't really *happen*. It was almost just *experienced*, and it's hard to say just what or why it happened that way.

I can tell you this. The first time I saw Benny Martin in years, you see, I remember when I was a little kid, the first time I saw him in years, he come over to my house drunk. Played "Lovesick Blues," singing loud. They couldn't wake me up because I'd been up all night before. He come by to get my mother to marry her. He wanted to get married and go out on the road that afternoon. So I went in and picked with him for a while. Then didn't see him again for about three months. And one night my mama ran into him out on the road and he turned around and followed her because he recognized the car.

A lot of it is because of Benny; that's how I met John [Hartford]. Lots happened. I've met lots of people through John, lots more through Benny. Certain amount of things like that at the Opry too. It's hard to say. And it's not really something I can easily relate.

SL: *Which bass players do you admire today?*
RH: Oh, that's a broad one. 'Cause there's so many now. Our union membership has doubled since I joined in '71. It's hard to say. Just about everybody plays something I like. I still kind of stick by the same ones I told you about earlier, Bob Moore, Strezlecki, Linneman, standbys. And like I said, there's jazz players like Ray Brown, David Holland, people like that.

SL: *Is the Nashville bluegrass and country scene changing?*
RH: You'd better believe it. Yes, actually right now the big thing seems to be bands of any type, to be a member of a band. Actual freelance session work, to be honest with you, isn't really quite the scale it used to be, because we do have so many bands, which in one way is bad for the session guys. They don't work like they used to, but it's good 'cause nobody hogs all the work. Everybody gets to work some. But it's changing an awful lot. It's changing, considerably, and it changes faster as the time's going on.

SL: *Is there more room for innovation right now in the music?*
RH: Some, of course, this has always been true too, some I think are too competition oriented. Competition I condone, backstabbing I really don't. I never have. My problem is, if you wonder how come I don't work any more than I do, I don't know if you want to put this down or not; please don't. I work enough, I make a living at it. But as far as politics and all, I'm not into that. I never have been. And there's quite a few reasons. A little politicking and just fun that may result in politicking, that's one thing. I don't go out specifically with that in mind. A lot of players do. A lot of players will show up at things for that reason. And I'm hard to even get out of the house. If you get me out of the house, it's usually to work and I then go back. If I am out, it's usually to have fun. And kind of screw the actual political scene.

SL: *Do you hang out at the Station Inn or other places?*
RH: Not a whole lot. I don't have a real hangout. Once in a while I might drop by or something.

SL: *Do you go and sit in?*
RH: Not very often, no. And half the time if I am there I almost prefer that people don't know I'm out there, for that reason. I go to see them, I don't get up and play my stuff. I want to hear the band.

SL: *Any hobbies?*

RH: Well, we've got two kids. One's three and one's five. Their names are J. T. and Tater Bug. J. T. is John Thomas and Tater Bug is Taylor Andrew. My wife's name is Lisa. We have been married since 1979, July of that year. We had known each other for over, well, a couple of years before that. We've been together for some time. We've got a pretty good thing going. She just says I keep too many cars. I think we're down to, let's see, five. I'm kind of into old cars.

I've got three old Cadillacs, a rope-shaft swing-axle Tempest. We've got the GS and the Battle Bomb. [The GS is] a '72 Buick with scoops in the hood that goes real fast. And the Battle Bomb is a battle bomb; it's pretty well self-explanatory. It's a car you could take down on lower Broad and no one will touch. I guarantee you even guys in New York would run from that thing. They wouldn't touch that dirty-lookin' thing for nothing. Pieces of the top peeled back flap in the air as you go down the road. I can leave a lot of money's worth of instruments in the car, and no one will touch it, because of the nature of the car. Not in that thing. They don't even want to look at it, let alone look in it.

SL: *Comment on some of the artists with whom you've worked. John Hartford?*
RH: He's great; I love [to work with him]. John is one who's very understanding if anything goes wrong. And he's certainly colorful 'cause you never know what he's going to say or do next. He's a lot of fun being in restaurants with 'cause you don't know what he's going to write on napkins. He loves to sit and write music on napkins, or draw on napkins or just write words, anything.

SL: *Does he leave it behind on the table or take it with him?*
RH: Either way. Sometimes people sitting at the table want to take it. Sometimes he just leaves it there, leaves it, then overtips the waitress.

SL: *Another colorful character, Peter Rowan?*

RH: Ooooh, colorful ain't the word for it. I guess that fits as good as any. It'd be hard to say. On the plane Pete's on, it's almost a spiritual thing for him constantly. It adds a lot of heart to his music. That's one thing in particular I enjoy about working for him. He is full at everything I've ever seen him do. He could throw a rock across the river and he'll put his heart into it.

SL: *Benny Martin?*
RH: You got about three more of these cassettes? I'll tell you some Benny Martin stories. I first have to comment on his personality. Right now Benny is somewhat more laid back than he used to be. He is a lot more laid back. Now, let's see. Try and describe Benny. Unpredictable, artistic, rather hotheaded about things. He knows what he wants and that's why he's this way. His ideas are good and being the artist he is, he definitely can state what he wants. I'm sure it's led him to clashes with other people. It's been a lot of his thing. He's worked with a lot of these other people. He worked with Lester and Bill, Earl. He's worked with all of them. He worked with Acuff.

SL: *How about Acuff?*
RH: Oh, Lord, now he's a hard one to describe. Acuff's almost really what you see. Very genuine, yes. Just about all the people you've asked me about though, this really fits to. He's always been like this. My dad worked with him. For about two years they traveled the road together. And Acuff is one of the most genuine people, very heartfelt in what he does. That really kind of describes it without going into individual instances. Things he said and things he does. If he tells you to do something, more than likely it's something he does. He doesn't tell people to do things he wouldn't do.

SL: *How about Bill Monroe?*
RH: Well now, I'll be honest with you. I don't know Bill that well. But I know Bill well enough. We had known each other kind of name-wise for years. We really didn't know each other 'til we

worked together a little bit. Bill, as everyone knows, he doesn't really talk a lot unless he knows you extremely well. And then again I think Bill would really rather talk with music a lot of the times. He's another one like Acuff, that's just another one of those really genuine souls that will generally tell you what he would do.

SL: *One more, Vassar Clements?*
RH: *(Clears his throat stifling a chuckle.)* He's a character, for sure, one of the livest senses of humor I think I've ever seen! Every one of these guys, incidentally, has their own brand of humor, none like the other. Vassar is definitely one of those guys. A musical perfectionist. One who I found isn't really an over-rehearser, which I like. He likes spontaneity. And he likes spontaneity not only in his music, but he likes spontaneity in everything. He likes it just as it happens. He's a lot of fun to be with.

SL: *Describe yourself.*
RH: Describe myself? Hmmmmm?? Confused, haphazard, a little bit nuts. I like to have fun. Extremely schizophrenic. I can change my moods quickly. Not always at will, but I'm subject to change quick. I'm funny about my work. One way that I can describe myself is that I'll work just about anything because I went too many years of knowing want, so I will try to work all I can. That's why I try to help people a lot and all 'cause I know what it's like to be there. I'm definitely a kind of a homebody, I guess, basically. But I do like to have a certain amount of fun, too. Most musicians will find me bland as hell probably. Until I get into playing some practical jokes on 'em. Then they'll be mad.

SL: *What would you be doing if you weren't recording and performing?*
RH: What would I be doing? Let me see. I would love to work with antique cars and such. If I wasn't into bass in particular, there are several other instruments I would like. I've always wanted to play piano. I do enjoy working with old cars. It's really hard to say

because since I got into music, I really haven't had many other aspirations like that.

SL: *Is there anything you would like to add?*
RH: I've enjoyed this immensely. You have been a lot of fun sitting here jawing with you. I've really had quite a lot of fun here. Hello Lisa, J. T., Tater Bug, Akk Akk, Putt, Crunchy, Squishy *(these last four are the family cats)*. Hello, Mama. Hello, Steve; that's my brother.

SL: *Will you play music all your life?*
RH: You're damned right I will *(laughs gently)*.

—ROY M. HUSKEY / 1956–1997

John Hartford (left) and Peter Rowan. Each was often accompanied by Roy on bass. The Bottom Line, New York City, November 9, 1984.

★ ★ ★

JOHN HARTFORD ON HUSKEY

HEARING IN COLORS

There was a subtle intuitive musical chemistry between John Hartford and Roy Huskey, witnessed in few such pairings. The mutual respect these two extraordinary musician friends had is reflected in the words of each describing the other.

Roy Huskey had a special ability: he heard notes in colors; that is, each musical note had an associative color in his mind. It's a phenomenon not uncommon and is a form of synesthesia. Synesthesia occurs when one sense perceives a stimulus as if it were perceived by another sense.

While Roy and I did not discuss his hearing in colors in the 1985 interview, his friend John Hartford provided some insight a few years after Roy passed away. I interviewed John in his home in Madison, Tennessee, March 13, 2000, for what turned out to be his last published interview before he died the following year. It appeared in the summer 2001 issue of *Sing Out!* magazine. At that time, in initial preparation for this book, we also spent a few minutes talking about Roy, with plans to talk further in the future, which was not to be. One gets a good picture of John himself in his own words, as well, from the humor that was in evidence as he reminisced about Roy.

SL: *If you could sum up the man and the musicianship of Roy Huskey, what words would you use to describe him and his music?*

JH: He was the best. I think he may be one of the best natural musicians I ever met. He was so good! I sent him up to Jack Clement, and Jack Clement said, "Now I can start making records again!" Roy had a real nice, friendly, generous personality. He was real easy to be around. Genuine.

SL: *Can you provide a little insight into Roy's ability to hear in colors?*
JH: Roy told me [that] for a long time, he didn't tell anybody that the notes were different colors, because he didn't want people to think he was crazy. He had perfect pitch. I've got it written down, like B-flat is black and C is white, [what] he told me about all this. We sat down one time and I made a color wheel and we made the [musical] scale. We wrote down the colors and he told me what color [corresponded to which note] and I wrote it all out. Some of them are just colors turning into other colors and others were like basic primary colors.

I was in a college bookstore somewhere, might have been Kansas or Nebraska. And there was a music book in there for a college class. It said the first, earliest known musical notation was the notes found in the abbeys the monks used in prayers and other things. It said that the earliest musical notation was in color and it listed the colors. And it was in fact the very same colors that Roy had told me. I should have bought that book. I just read that and I was so amazed. Roy and I had just been talking about that. He might have been out on the bus asleep when that happened; I don't remember because he and I used to travel *a lot*. I happened to have a 3 x 5 card in my pocket [and wrote down what I read].

Sometimes [now] I think he's on the bus. I'll be walking down the hall in the middle of the night and I'll think Roy's up there in the bunk snoring away. And I'll say, "Roy, you got a bad case of bunk head!" *(John laughs.)* He'd call himself bunk head.

I hear textures in notes. Some of them are furry and some of them are sweet, almost like stainless steel. C is like G, but first thing in the morning *(laughs)*. C is G first thing in the morning. He gets up and he's "ceeeeee." And then in the middle as the day progresses, well, about one o'clock in the afternoon, it becomes "geeeeeeeeeee."

Anyhow, I don't remember what he said G was. I'm pretty sure C is white, A is red and B-flat is black. He told Lisa that he had a dream that, if he was at the end of the universe, that the last sound the universe made before it ceased to be was the note B-flat. One B-flat and then it was all over *(laughs)*.

He came over to the *Julia Belle Swain* one time and we got to blowing the whistle. And we got to writing down what it was because it had a big long arm on it, had all these great chromatic notes *(makes a sound like whewwwweeeeeeeuuuuu)*, a steam whistle. Roy could write down where all the chords were as they changed through this. "The steam out there on the side is A-flat." Well, my God, to be, to have all that . . . He was just as easygoing, a natural guy, you would've thought . . . This boy plays by ear, just happens to be real good, but he's real easy to play with and friendly.

He had an ear where he could tell *(John knocks on several items in the room)* kind of like boom boom, "Oh, this room is E-flat," in other words, if the strings were low enough so that he would hear one string being a little more resonant than anything else. He'll know where in a room to stand to take advantage of that. So he's barely touching those strings and they sound like he's tearing them off the thing.

In fact he told me something, I don't know for sure he said this, but I think one time he told me that, boy, now I'm going to go out on a limb when I say this, maybe you ought to get it down 'cause at least it's a rumor of what he said.

He had a certain bass, I think it was Brownie, which was the bass that his daddy came to Nashville with [when he was with] Lester Flatt and Earl Scruggs, or actually his daddy came with Carl Smith. And Brownie had a real good G on it. You know, when you're playing a Foggy Mountain Boy bass, it's got a lot of tunes in G. And he said that the new Opry house, not the Ryman Auditorium, but the new Opry house, had a resonance of G that was too much; it threw everything out of balance. So he had to be real careful about taking Brownie down there. He took this other bass that had a resonance of a different frequency, so he could have better control over the room when he was playing.

And he said that *(laughs)*—we used to get pretty far out in our discussions—I believe he said one time that he thought that was the reason bluegrass didn't sound as good in the new Opry house as it did in the old Opry house because the room had such low resonance. And if you think about it and if you listen to what goes out over there, it doesn't have the sound that the Ryman does. First time he ever heard Ed Haley, he said, "Now that's the old-fashioned intonation." He loved Ed Haley. He could hear Ed Haley. To the average guy, Ed sounds like he's playing out of tune. But old Roy could hear it. He said, "That's way back up in there." Oh, man . . .

Those are some fond memories. I really miss him, I'll tell you what. Roy and I invented the kitty goosers *(laughing)*. Except we started out in French, we called it "kitty goo-say." That's just what happens when you've stayed up too long. In fact, we wrote a song about it called "The Old Kitty Goosing." We have to start looking for kittens to goose . . . *(laughs)*.

—JOHN HARTFORD / 1937–2001

* See page 77 for photos of Roy and John.

Above: Guitarist and storyteller Gamble Rogers. Gamble, a former member of the Serendipity Singers, died in 1991 while trying to save a person who was drowning. "He left this world holding out his hand." (*Song for Gamble* by Charles John Quarto and Steve Gillette.) A Folk Celebration, Carnegie Hall, New York City, May 17, 1985.

Right: Eileen Carson (left) and Amy Sarli of the Fiddle Puppet Dancers. A clog dance shoe with a microphone placed in it to pick up the sound of the tap steps can be discerned on the stage just in front of Eileen's feet near the bottom of the photo. Waterloo Bluegrass Festival, Waterloo Village, Stanhope, New Jersey, August 24, 1985.

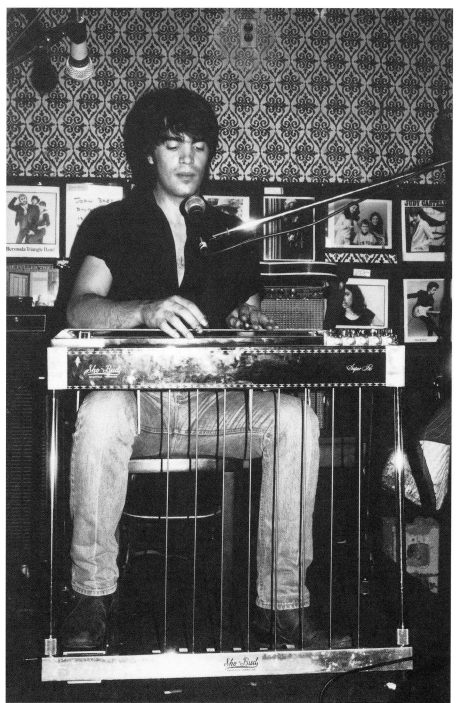

Above: Little Roy Lewis of the Lewis Family, the "First Family of Bluegrass Gospel." Waterloo Bluegrass Festival, Waterloo Village, Stanhope, New Jersey, August 1985.

Right: Larry Campbell swings on pedal steel during a show with the Happy Traum Band. Interesting to note are the images in the background lining the wall of the legendary club—early promo photos and handbills, a virtual history of folk and popular music of that era. Over Larry's right shoulder is a placeholder regarding a missing Joan Baez photo. Gerdes Folk City, New York City, August 7, 1983.

Above: Ralph Stanley and the Clinch Mountain Boys play to a packed pavilion. From left, long-time Stanley bassist Jack Cooke, John Rigsby on mandolin, Ralph Stanley II, his son Nathan Stanley standing behind the line, Ralph Stanley, Steve Sparkman on banjo, guitarist James Allen Shelton, fiddler James Price. Delaware Valley Bluegrass Festival, Woodstown, New Jersey, September 1, 2001.

Right: Bluegrass and traditional singer Hazel Dickens joined by Dudley Connell, former member of the Johnson Mountain Boys and now lead singer for the Seldom Scene. Earl Yeager, another former Johnson Mountain Boy, is in the background playing bass. Kean College's Little Theater, Union, New Jersey, March 18, 1990.

Green Grass Cloggers. Visible in the lower right, accompanying musicians include Raymond W. McLain on fiddle and Michael McLain on banjo. Under Raymond's left arm is a dobro which was played by Jerry Douglas. The rest of the backup band, not visible, included Sharon White on guitar, Mark Hembree on bass, and Buck White on mandolin. The Cloggers are ("sort of" left to right) the leg of Phil Jamison, Tricia Cook (yellow dress), Gordy Hinners (frontmost male dancer), Andy Deaver (green dress), Cherie Sheppard (blue dress), Van King in red-and-white shirt. The Green Grass Cloggers were founded in 1971 and changed personnel many times over the years. They introduced choreographed routines based on four-couple western square dance figures, unlike the freestyle clogging done by traditional teams of the era. In 1972 and 1974 they took world championship honors at the prestigious Fiddler's Grove in North Carolina. They continue to perform today with a reunion team of dancers. McLain Family Festival, Big Hill Farm near Berea, Kentucky, August 1982.

Bill Monroe. Lincoln Center Out-of-Doors Festival,
Damrosch Park, New York City, August 23, 1987.

A legendary profile in silhouette.

Preceding page: From the end of June and into the first couple of weeks of July 1982, I drove from New York City to Washington, D.C., into Virginia and on down to North Carolina, with a return trip via Pennsylvania—all the while stopping at various and sundry places for music. First stop was the Smithsonian for its Festival of American Folklife. A Woody Guthrie tribute concert was held June 25 and among the participants were Arlo Guthrie, Studs Terkel, Bernice Reagon, Josh White, Jr., Ronnie Gilbert, and Pete Seeger. I was shooting from side stage and realized a whole different perspective being projected onto the sound truck parked behind the staging platform. So far no "folkie" I know has failed to identify Pete Seeger, including Pete himself, and his trademark long-necked banjo in silhouette. Shown on this page (left) is Pete pictured "in the flesh," from which I grabbed the shadow image. Above: Josh White, Jr., and Ronnie Gilbert of the Weavers look on while awaiting turns to offer songs during the Woody Guthrie tribute.

Above: Frank Wakefield picks mandolin alongside John Herald at the New York City Bluegrass Festival, Snug Harbor Cultural Center, Staten Island, New York, June 23, 1984.

Top right: A reunion of the Greenbriar Boys (left to right) John Herald, Ralph Rinzler, Bob Yellin. Lincoln Center Out-of-Doors Festival, Damrosch Park, New York City, August 24, 1986.

Bottom right: Backstage I caught Pete Seeger conferring with festival director and former Greenbriar Boy Ralph Rinzler, along with Arlo Guthrie. Festival of American Folklife, Washington, D.C., June 25, 1982.

A quick history lesson to tie these photographs together: Ralph Rinzler left the Greenbriar Boys and went on to found and direct the Festival of American Folklife (now called the Smithsonian Folklife Festival) until his death in 1994. Frank Wakefield took his place in the Greenbriar Boys.

Members of Johnnie Lee Wills and his Western Swing Band. Pictured is pedal steel player Jack Rider; Glenn "Blub" Reese is in the background on saxophone. Festival of American Folklife, Washington, D.C., June 26, 1982.

Above: Luce Amen, winner of the Marlboro Country Music Local Talent Roundup. Madison Square Garden, New York City, May 21, 1988.

Right: Chris Thile of Nickel Creek. *Time* magazine named the youthful group "a musical innovator for the new millennium." Philadelphia Folk Festival, Schwenksville, Pennsylvania, August 25, 2001.

JOHNSON MOUNTAIN BOYS

NOT AT THE OLD SCHOOLHOUSE

During the mid-eighties, while living in New York City, I dabbled in the occasional booking of a bluegrass or folk group in a couple of the local music clubs where I had previously established a rapport as a music journalist. In late 1987, I took the big plunge when the now long-gone but still legendary Lone Star Café, located on Fifth Avenue at Thirteenth Street, agreed to let me produce a monthly Sunday bluegrass series. The Lone Star made for an unusual setting, both aurally and photographically, because it was a converted Schraft's ice cream parlor; entering through the revolving front door, the bar area was on the immediate left, while the stage platform was directly across from it, with only about four feet of space between them, including bar stools. Some of the best seats in the house were up above in the balcony, reached by a set of stairs just beyond and to one side of the stage. The stairs, as well as the balcony, provided atypical vantage points for photography.

The first concert I booked there was the Johnson Mountain Boys.

Shortly before the date, the band, in spite of their tremendous popularity on the bluegrass circuit, announced their impending breakup. Much to my astonishment as well as to the Lone Star management's, four hundred fans turned out, filling the club to capacity; we had hoped for two hundred. It was December 6, 1987.

It was a hectic but exciting night. The cook hadn't yet shown up, so the manager was flipping burgers furiously. I was busy getting the concert under way, emceeing, greeting friends and fans. I had, of course, brought my cameras along. But in the frenzy, I shot off a roll without realizing it never wound onto the spool. Thank goodness for second sets. I reloaded and took another roll.

When I reviewed the slides, one particular frame caught my eye for its unmistakable representation of bluegrass gospel singing—a shot from behind of the backs of the singers' heads, that is, "the hats" gathered around a single mic to harmonize. I knew Rounder Records had a "final" album in the works for the Johnson Mountain Boys and so

I approached them about using the "hats" photo, thinking it would make a great back cover graphic. They asked me to send it and some other "JMB" photos for consideration.

Imagine my surprise and delight when I found a message on my answering machine from Rounder stating that they didn't want to use the "hats" on the back cover, but asking if it would be okay if they used one of my other shots on the front cover. The album is *The Johnson Mountain Boys: At the Old Schoolhouse*, recorded live in Lucketts, Virginia; it was the 1990 International Bluegrass Music Association (IBMA) Record of the Year and a 1989 Grammy Award finalist for Bluegrass Album of the Year.

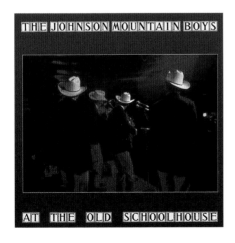

Left: Album cover reproduced by permission of Rounder Records.

Above: Johnson Mountain Boys, Lone Star Café, New York City, December 6, 1987.

Left: Contemporary singer-songwriter Tom Chapin. In addition to performing his own material, Tom, along with other Chapin family members, continues to keep the music and humanitarian causes of his brother, Harry, alive and in the public eye. Buccleuch Park, New Brunswick, New Jersey, July 19, 2001.

Above: Barachois, who performed the traditional music and dance of Canada's Island Acadians, with a comedic twist. Audience members' heads are transformed into percussion instruments being brushed and banged upon by Albert Arsenault. The group retired at the end of 2003. Delaware Valley Bluegrass Festival, Woodstown, New Jersey, August 30, 2002.

Above: New Grass Revival's John Cowan. Lone Star Café, New York City, August 8, 1984.

Right: Cowan and New Grass Revival founding member Sam Bush (back to camera) harmonize. New York City Bluegrass Festival, Snug Harbor Cultural Center, Staten Island, New York, June 30, 1985.

Doc Watson. With only harmonica
accompaniment, Doc encores with
"Dixie." The Bottom Line, New York
City, September 14, 1986.

Roy Clark performs while Roy Acuff
looks on. Grand Ole Opry, Nashville,
Tennessee, October 11, 1986.

Steve Riley fronting his Mamou Play-
boys. Due to the height of the stage
and my own lack of height, I had to
balance precariously on a wobbly
folding chair to grab this photo. Craw-
fish Fest, Waterloo Village, Stanhope,
New Jersey, June 5, 1999.

A cappella gospel harmonizing: the Fairfield Four and the Nashville Bluegrass Band. Both groups participated in the music projects associated with the two films *O Brother, Where Art Thou?* and *Down from the Mountain*. International Bluegrass Music Association Awards Show, River-Park Center, Owensboro, Kentucky, September 24, 1992.

Left: Traditional musicians Norman and Nancy Blake. Norman provided the memorable rendition of "You Are My Sunshine" as well as a moving instrumental arrangement of "I Am a Man of Constant Sorrow" for the *O Brother, Where Art Thou?* soundtrack. Delaware Valley Bluegrass Festival, Woodstown, New Jersey, August 30, 2002.

Above: Bill Harrell, one of the most distinctive voices in bluegrass. Prospect Park Bandshell, Brooklyn, New York, August 10, 1984.

Left: Jack Lawrence, Doc Watson's picking partner since the early eighties. Delaware Valley Bluegrass Festival, Woodstown, New Jersey, September 5, 1998.

Above: Multi-instrumentalist (and multi-tattooed) Jimmy Arnold. New York City Bluegrass Festival, Snug Harbor Cultural Center, Staten Island, New York, June 30, 1985.

Above and left: John Hartford and Roy Huskey, looking for the perfect notes, which they always found together. The Bottom Line, New York City, June 12, 1986.

Opposite page: The prolific composer of "Gentle on My Mind," John Hartford was a consummate musician and entertainer. His onstage persona was captivating in a humble way, as modest as the man behind the mic. In his last published interview, which appeared in *Sing Out!* magazine, he responded to how he wanted to be remembered by others: "I have no control over that; I'm doing what's in my heart. If it works, that's great. If it doesn't work, at least I haven't wasted my time." Waterloo Folk Festival, Waterloo Village, Stanhope, New Jersey, September 3, 1984.

Left: Contemporary singer-songwriter Claudia Schmidt. Philadelphia Folk Festival, Schwenksville, Pennsylvania, August 27, 1989.

Above: Fiddlin' Tex Logan eclipses "hillbilly jazz" fiddler Vassar Clements behind him to his left. Silver Cloud Music Festival, Rondout Valley Resort, Accord, New York, September 10, 1983.

Multi-genre songwriter-singer Peter Rowan (right) and with conga player Kester Smith (above). Midnight Jam, Merle Watson Memorial Festival (now called MerleFest), Wilkesboro, North Carolina, May 1, 1993.

Above: David "Dawg" Grisman. The Bottom Line, New York City, July 15, 1985.

Left: John Jorgenson, co-founder of the Desert Rose Band. The Bottom Line, New York City, August 13, 1987.

Above: The Country Gentlemen 25th Anniversary Reunion. Seen here (from left to right) are Bluegrass Unlimited's founder/editor Pete Kuyk-endall, a.k.a. Pete Roberts (banjo), Tom Gray (bass), Eddie Adcock (banjo), John Duffey (mandolin), Charlie Waller (guitar). The Country Gentlemen changed the face of bluegrass, initiating the progressive bluegrass move-ment with their folk style renditions and "outside the realm" repertoire. Wolf Trap Farm Park for the Performing Arts, Vienna, Virginia, July 5, 1982.

Right: One-half of the English traditional duo of John Roberts (pictured) and Tony Barrand. Philadelphia Folk Festival, Schwenksville, Pennsylvania, August 27, 1989.

Above: Jimmie Dale Gilmore and Joe Ely, who, along with Butch Hancock, perform hot country music as The Flatlanders. Philadelphia Folk Festival, Schwenksville, Pennsylvania, August 25, 2002.

Riders in the Sky demonstrate "the cowboy way." (Right) Ranger Doug appears amazed, perhaps at Too Slim's face-playing abilities (above) or maybe at Woody Paul's lariat-twirling talents (opposite page). The Bottom Line, New York City, February 4, 1988.

Above: Wretched Refuse String Band. A bluegrass-old time-Catskill "schtick" band. Left to right: Quadruple fiddle threats Alan Kaufman, Marty Laster, Citizen Kafka, a.k.a. Richard Shulberg, Kenny Kosek, guitarists Jon Sholle and Bob Jones. The Bottom Line, New York City, January 20, 1991.

Left: Fiddle Fever featuring (left to right) Matt Glaser, Jay Ungar, Molly Mason (bass), Evan Stover. Russ Barenberg is outside this frame playing guitar. Triplex Theater, Borough of Manhattan Community College, New York City, March 10, 1985.

Piedmont blues legend and National Heritage Fellowship recipient John Jackson. This was the last time I saw John. He and his personal manager, Trish Byerly, had befriended me in the early nineties when I was coordinating John's appearance for a local organization. At that time, John, well into his seventies, had recently learned how to write and proudly signed one of his CDs for me. Later, in my capacity as director of the New Jersey Folk Festival, I had booked a return engagement for him to appear at the April 2002 event. But he passed away unexpectedly in January of that year after a brief bout with cancer. The black-and-white shot seen here was subsequently incorporated into the festival's 2002 logo, appearing on the program book, T-shirts, and promotional posters. The photo choice was not mine but that of the Rutgers University students who manage the event. When considering the photo, they were unaware that it was the image of the recently deceased headliner and that I had taken the shot. Clearwater's Hudson River Revival, Croton Point Park, Croton-on-Hudson, New York, June 1999.

Above: Bluegrass jams are famous for occurring in many an unlikely place. In recent years a number of multi-day bluegrass events have moved indoors during the cooler seasons. This picking session occurred in the lobby of the historic Galt House hotel during the International Bluegrass Music Association's World of Bluegrass. Louisville, Kentucky, September 30, 2003.

Right: Pam Gadd, a successful songwriter, when she was a member of the New Coon Creek Girls. Bassist Vicki Simmons is to her right. Wind Gap (Pennsylvania) Bluegrass Festival, June 1986.

Above: John McEuen of the Nitty Gritty Dirt Band guests with Russian bluegrass band Kukuruza. Shown with McEuen are lead singer Irina Surina and guitarist Michael Venhkov. International Bluegrass Music Association Awards Show, RiverPark Center, Owensboro, Kentucky, September 24, 1992.

Left: Perhaps one of the most dynamic concerts I ever attended was the one put on by Milladoiro from Spain. With the Celtic-infused traditional folk sounds of their home region of Galicia, the energy and synergy among them was electrifying. Ritz Theatre, Elizabeth, New Jersey, November 6, 1993.

Above and right: "King of Country Music" Roy Acuff and comedienne Minnie Pearl. 61st Birthday Celebration of the Grand Ole Opry, Nashville, Tennessee, October 11, 1986.

Opposite page: Stage 1 of the Walnut Valley Festival is observed through the haze during a performance of "superpicker" progressive bluegrass group The Grass Is Greener. Fans call this premier festival a "picker's paradise." On stage are Tony Trischka (banjo), Richard Greene (fiddle), Buell Neidlinger (bass), David Grier (guitar), Butch Baldassari (mandolin). Winfield, Kansas, September 1996.

"Zydeco" Queen Ida. Zydeco music takes its name from the Creole French word for "snap bean," a reference to the rhythmic "snapping" beat of the highly danceable music. Philadelphia Folk Festival, Schwenksville, Pennsylvania, August 26, 1989.

Left: The McLain Family Band: Michael McLain, Raymond K. McLain, Michael Riopel, Nancy Ann McLain, Ruth McLain Riopel, Raymond W. McLain. The group toured around the world, performing in sixty-two countries in addition to all fifty states in this country. Seasoned, dedicated entertainers who always showed their appreciation of fans and friends, the McLains went on with this show in spite of having just learned of the death of their grandfather. New York University Loeb Student Center, New York City, May 2, 1981.

Above: Doc Watson. Waterloo Folk Festival, Waterloo Village, Stanhope, New Jersey, September 3, 1984.

Pat Cannon (yellow dress) and her Foot and Fiddle Dance Company: Germaine Goodson (blue dress), Debbie Thomas (facing camera), and Margaret Morrison (obscured). Queens Bluegrass Festival, Queens Farm, Floral Park, New York, August 16, 1986.

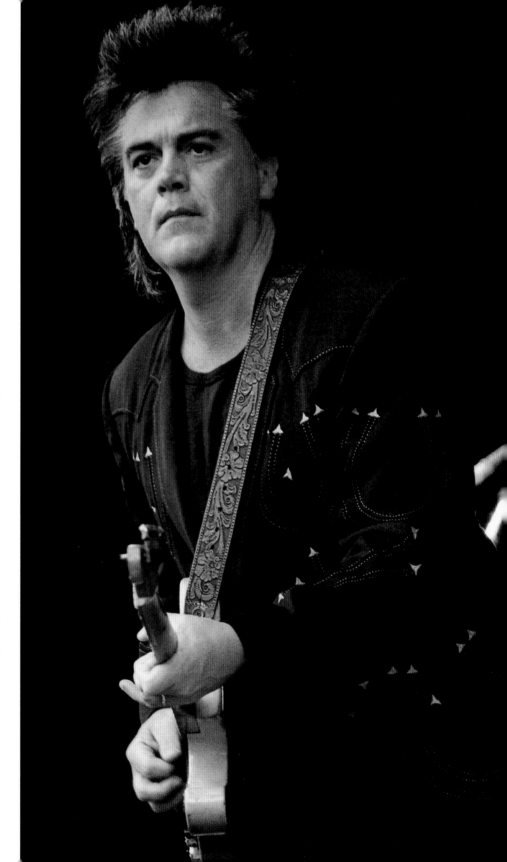

★ ★ ★

MARTY STUART ON LESTER FLATT

Marty Stuart was among the first major bluegrass musicians I met. We had not seen each other in a while when he appeared for a number of New York City area dates with Peter Rowan and an entourage of hot pickers. Among the gigs was an appearance at the Vernon Valley Bluegrass Festival, July 29, 1984, where Peter was joined by Marty, banjo picker Bill Keith, fiddler Mark O'Connor, and bass player Roy Huskey. Bill Monroe was also on the program, and he stepped up to the microphone and did a couple of songs with this ensemble, too. (I documented these moments in photos. But this festival stage was a challenging one, an open deck high above the ground at a former ski resort. I was braver than most, doing a strange balancing act all too near the unprotected edge to grab some of the photos. Memorable shots, yes; outstanding photographs, unfortunately, no.)

After the set, Marty and I sat down and chatted, not for an interview, but as old friends. He asked me candidly what I thought of his latest solo album, *Busy Bee Cafe* (it's wonderful). A member of Johnny Cash's band at the time, Marty told me about his own, which he had formed and with whom he had worked a handful of performances in recent weeks. Marty Stuart and the Rhythm Kings played a blend of country rock, rockabilly, and bluegrass, he explained. But Marty was quick to emphasize that "first and foremost I am a bluegrass musician. Anything I do has been added on to that. I'll never lose the effect Lester Flatt [had on me]."

[93]   Marty Stuart. Philadelphia Folk Festival, Schwenksville, Pennsylvania, August 25, 2002.

Above: Jackie Daly of Ireland's Patrick Street.
Philadelphia Folk Festival, Schwenksville,
Pennsylvania, August 27, 1989.

Right: The Smith Sisters, Debi and Megan,
playing Appalachian dulcimer in duet. The
Bottom Line, New York City, June 4, 1987.

The John Cowan Band with guests Sam Bush on electric mandolin to the right of Cowan (middle of photo in red shirt), and Led Zeppelin guitarist John Paul Jones to Cowan's left. Band members from left to right are banjo player Rex McGee, young fiddle ace Luke Bulla, guitarist Jeff Autry, and Wayne Benson, mandolin. MerleFest, Wilkesboro, North Carolina, May 1, 2004.

Above: John Hartford wanders into the audience while fiddling. Waterloo Folk Festival, Waterloo Village, Stanhope, New Jersey, September 3, 1984.

Right: John Hartford clogging on his dance board while he plays. The Bottom Line, New York City, February 22, 1985.

Opposite page: "King of Bluegrass" Jimmy Martin, with Audie Blaylock, mandolin, and Chris Warner, banjo. Waterloo Bluegrass Festival, Waterloo Village, Stanhope, New Jersey, August 1986.

Country star Emmylou Harris. Lone Star
Café, New York City, August 29, 1986.

Folk songster Tom Paxton with flatpicking champion Steve Kaufman (partially obscured). Walnut Valley Festival, Winfield, Kansas, September 1996.

Wynonna Judd (above) when she was still appearing as a duo with her mother, Naomi. Country superstar Randy Travis (left and opposite). Marlboro Country Music Tour '88, Madison Square Garden, New York City, May 21, 1988.

Above: John McEuen. The stage spotlights would be turned off and John would light sparklers affixed to his guitar's peghead. The Bottom Line, New York City, July 15, 1985.

Top left: The Seldom Scene's John Duffey behind the flashy specs with T. Michael Coleman to his left in the shadows. The Bottom Line, New York City, June 3, 1988.

Bottom left: Little Roy Lewis is famous, or infamous, for his onstage gags during sets by other artists. Here he dons his Lady Liberty headgear for a few laughs. Wind Gap (Pennsylvania) Bluegrass Festival, June 1986.

Opposite page: Red Knuckles and the Trailblazers, the zany, colorfully outfitted country swing alter ego of the progressive bluegrass group Hot Rize. From left, Red Knuckles, Wendell Mercantile, Slade. Just beyond the frame is Waldo Otto. The Bottom Line, New York City, June 12, 1986.

Above: Songwriter Eric Andersen ("Thirsty Boots," "Ghosts Upon the Road") backed by songwriter-guitarist-producer John Leventhal. Leventhal is noted for his work with Shawn Colvin, Jim Lauderdale, and wife Rosanne Cash. The Bottom Line, New York City, December 3, 1988.

Right: Fiddle Puppet Dancers Eileen Carson (facing camera) and Amy Sarli are joined by Rodney Sutton for some hamboning and play-party songs. Waterloo Bluegrass Festival, Waterloo Village, Stanhope, New Jersey, August 24, 1985.

Above: In a somewhat rare appearance together, half-brothers Mike (left) and Pete Seeger (right) share a pensive moment on stage. At left, Pete gestures animatedly while relating a story. What made these photos a bit unusual was that once I took my fourth-row aisle seat, I never left it to shoot off this roll; I had managed to sit in probably the best "photography" seat in the house. Virginia Festival of the Book, University of Virginia, Culbreth Theatre, Charlottesville, Virginia, March 21, 2001.

Above: Grandpa Jones, for many years one of
the stars of *Hee Haw*. 61st Birthday Celebration
of the Grand Ole Opry, Nashville, Tennessee,
October 11, 1986.

Right: Utah Phillips. Philadelphia Folk Festival,
Schwenksville, Pennsylvania, August 2001.

Audie Blaylock "rages" with bluegrass
superstar Rhonda Vincent. Delaware
Valley Bluegrass Festival, Woodstown,
New Jersey, September 1, 2001.

★ ★ ★

THE BOTTOM LINE WAS TOPS

Two friends, Allan Pepper and Stanley Snadowsky, opened the doors on February 12, 1974, to a new club, a concept. Their goal, in their own words, was "to create a music room, not a jazz, rock or folk club but a venue where many different genres could find an audience," and where the focus would always be on the music.

For nearly thirty years, the Bottom Line in New York City was a showcase for both the legendary and legends-in-waiting. Like the menu of a twenty-four-hour diner, the lineup provided something for everyone: singer-songwriters, traditional folk, blues, bluegrass, country, string band, Cajun, Celtic, klezmer, folk-rock, and much more. Bagpipes, banjos, fiddles, and flutes all could be heard, played by some of the most formidable practitioners in the world. Among the hundreds who called the club "home" for a night were David Bromberg, Doc Watson, Christine Lavin, John Hartford, Stephane Grappelli, Taj Mahal, Alison Krauss and Union Station, Nanci Griffith, Asleep At The Wheel, Loudon Wainwright III, Battlefield Band, and Tom Chapin.

Sadly, the Bottom Line shut its doors on January 22, 2004, forced to close due to a variety of circumstances. As of this writing, the co-owners were investigating alternate sites in anticipation of reopening.

Just as the Station Inn in Nashville is a mecca, the Bottom Line was the Big Apple's. I was fortunate to have spent many a long night there, listening and photographing. I even took my lumps there, like the night someone whacked me in the head with a flying magazine when I apparently—and inadvertently—stepped into his view while photographing.

Or the night I came out of the club around 2:30 in the morning to find my car window smashed to bits and the shattered glass littering the driver's seat. I was horrified when, *with their bare hands*, guitarist Merle Watson and bass player T. Michael Coleman came to my rescue and picked up and swept away the glass pieces!

Interesting memories among the hundreds of musical moments in my mind and captured through my lens. I look forward to returning to a new Bottom Line location. In the meantime, take a nostalgic trip through the years with those photographs in this book that were snapped there.

Progressive bluegrass group Hot Rize. Left to right: Pete
Wernick, Nick Forster, Tim O'Brien, Charles Sawtelle.
The Bottom Line, New York City, June 12, 1986.

Above: Peter Ecklund, appearing with Jay Ungar, Molly Mason and Swingology. Philadelphia Folk Festival, Schwenksville, Pennsylvania, August 25, 2001.

Right: Alan MacLeod, while with the Tannahill Weavers. The Bottom Line, New York City, September 19, 1984.

Left: Mark Fain, bassist for Ricky Skaggs and Kentucky Thunder. In the background, banjo player Jim Mills can be discerned. Bluegrass Fan Fest, Galt House, Louisville, Kentucky, October 2002.

Above: Sean Grissom, "Cajun Cello." First Annual Village Voice Festival of Street Entertainers, Astor Place, Greenwich Village, New York City, September 9, 1984.

The Soldier's Fancy. Left to right: Doreen D'Amico, Marie Mularczyk, Debra Cerruti, Jane Przybysz. This all-women ensemble was known for its tightly woven a cappella harmonies, as well as for multi-instrumental accompaniment on guitar, banjo, mandolin, dulcimer, bouzouki, drum, recorder, pennywhistle, spoons, and limberjack. First Annual Village Voice Festival of Street Entertainers, Astor Place, Greenwich Village, New York City, September 9, 1984.

★ ★ ★

JIMMIE SKINNER, GENTLEMAN SONGWRITER

After more than two years working at *Pickin'* magazine, I was hooked on bluegrass. Since it was still very early in my professional career, I also decided it was time for a change. So I picked up and moved from New Jersey to Nashville. And while I did not land a job "in the music," and eventually moved back to the East Coast, I did have the opportunity to pursue wonderful friendships and conversations with many great musicians and songwriters in bluegrass and country music.

Composer of such classics as "You Don't Know My Mind" and "Doin' My Time," Kentuckian Jimmie Skinner was a gentleman's gentleman. He gained notoriety first in early country music, only later to become known and widely recorded within the bluegrass field. Not only a songwriter and singer, he became a pioneer in the traditional music industry when he opened up his record store in Cincinnati, Ohio, making country, blues, and bluegrass available to the public on a wider basis than had been the case previously.

While I was living in Nashville, he and his wife, Betty, had me over for dinner from time to time, and on one such occasion we chatted, rambling and traveling over the highways of time in his career as one of the twentieth century's most prolific country and bluegrass songwriters. Here are a few highlights from that conversation, taped February 15, 1978, in Hendersonville, Tennessee.

EARLY MUSIC MEMORIES

When I was about seven or eight years old, I can remember the square dances we would have in Kentucky. My dad played a little bit of banjo. He won a banjo out of a big barrel of peanuts. He won this little banjo we called the peanut banjo. It was very small. I learned to play on this little banjo, and my older brother did, too. I learned to play fiddle, too. And I heard Jimmie Rodgers sing. It started from that. I was just born and raised up in music.

I always loved blues. I love any kind of blues, Jimmie Rodgers, the way he could yodel and I loved the way he strummed his guitar. I did learn a little bit of guitar like him. Of course, I can't yodel like him!

I sometimes pick up the banjo . . . [and] play a tune on the banjo, what they call frailing now. When I was a boy, it was just "pickin' the banjer." I like the fiddle and I have a fiddle here at home, but I could never learn to play the fiddle the way I wanted to.

The first song that I heard that I can remember that I liked real well was on an Edison record . . . a little round disc. I heard the "Blue Ridge Mountain Blues" on [the] gramophone. That was a song I really liked, but I had *not a dream* of ever doing this myself! But I loved this song and used to go around singing it whenever I'd go to school. I'd sing this song all the way.

"Let Me Sleep in Your Barn Tonight, Mister" was another classic that I knew. And I knew a little bit of a song called—it later came out as "Frankie and Johnny" by Jimmie Rodgers, but then it was called "Frankie and Albert" *(laughs heartily)*. Same melody and almost the same words. He just rewrote it as "Frankie and Johnny." So that was the first songs I heard that I liked.

I hadn't heard any popular music down home, except I can remember one song, called "My Blue Heaven," which was a big song. And another song called "It Ain't Going to Rain No More." But that was the only songs that I knew.

We had the "race" records they called them [back] then. They were the blues by the black artists. And I loved those records. I didn't know who was singing. We would order them from Sears, Roebuck. My dad loved blues. So we'd get those records. We didn't look at who the artists were. We just played the blues on the records.

[In school we would] sing in the morning. We'd open up the school and sing some hymns. I can recall the teacher called me out one time to lead the song and I couldn't do that. And he said, "Well, I can hear you because you're singing louder than anyone, so you can lead the song." But when they took all the rest of them away from me, I wouldn't do anything then. As long as I could sing with the group, I could sing real loud.

[Music] was a hobby; it was just what I loved. I had no idea that I would become a professional. I also played a harmonica, a little twenty-five-cent harmonica that I had to learn to play. When I'd go to school, I kept it hidden in an old hollow tree, part of the time, till I'd come out at recess and then I'd usually play some tunes on that. I loved all kinds of music. And I seemed to have the

Photo courtesy of Jimmie Skinner.

knack at that time of being able to learn a little bit about any kind of an instrument. I guess I just loved music.

FIRST SONGS

Then we moved to Ohio, we moved from Kentucky to Ohio. As I said, I heard in maybe '27, I guess I heard the records by Jimmie Rodgers. Then I began to think about that I would love to write a song. But I didn't think about the song for commercial purposes or anything. I thought I love this music, the way it phrases and everything. "I think I would like to write a song." That was in my mind for a long time.

And one day I was out in a cornfield; we would cut corn in the fall of the year. There wasn't much work then and I'd cut corn and get so much a "shock," get a dime a shock, make a dollar a day.

And one real beautiful September day, we had our lunch, me and my uncle, and I was going back to the cornfield and this nice breeze blowing and everything, and the wild geese flying over and all, this song came to my mind, my first song. I called it "Headin' South." I might have it on my next album. I've never recorded it. That day before I left the cornfield, as I went along the cornrow, shocking up this corn, I finished the little song. The whole thing as I went along. I just kept going over and over it, through the whole thing that entire afternoon. It stayed in my mind.

Sometimes a melody comes to me now and will just leave me if I'm out and don't have a tape recorder. I had a better memory then, I guess. The song was kind of simple, a little bluesy song. I kind of had the blues. I wanted to leave and come back to Kentucky. So I wrote my first song out in the cornfield. I guess I was in my kind of early teens. I don't know exactly, but it was before I was twenty years old. I'm sure of that.

FAILURE . . . THEN SUCCESS

The sun went down on me a lot of times before I ever did get into anything really where I was known. In Richmond, Indiana, they had Gennett Records. My brother played banjo and me and him would work together. I would do a little singing, he'd play the banjo, and I played the guitar. We went to this recording company. I guess that must have been in the late twenties, a little bit after Rodgers. We went over there for an audition. They wanted to know if we had any new songs. And I didn't know what they were talking about. I had the one [I had written], but I wouldn't dare sing it to anybody. So I said no. They said, "Well, we like your voice, but we want new material to record. We love your voice. It's good for recording." We cut two instrumentals that day. They were to be released in a couple of weeks. But that's about the time the Depression hit and . . . that went down the drain and the sun went down on us there. We didn't get the masters which I wish we had today, 'cause it was just me on guitar and my brother played the banjo on a couple of tunes, one of which he did record later. But that was the first time that I almost got into the record business. And that failed.

Well, I will say this. They wrote me and asked me if I could do a song called "Ninety-nine Years." That was shortly after a hit song called "Twenty-one Years" had come out. "Ninety-nine Years" was a follow-up to that. Gene Autry, I believe, had recorded the song. They wanted it for their label, Gennett did. They wanted to know if I knew the song. Well, I hadn't even heard it by that time. So that, of course, fell through. That would have been a chance, if I'd gone back and recorded that.

Nevertheless, I got into radio. To record was my greatest ambition. The radio didn't hold a lot of thrills for me. Even though I was on a lot of programs, it just didn't thrill me like making a record.

I made my first record on a label called Red Barn. Today this is a common thing, making your own records. At that time, it wasn't common. A man came to me and said, "Jimmie, make your own records." He told me how I could do this and pay for them. I didn't care; I paid. Anything to be on records. I did make the record. The first one, you wouldn't believe, I think was "Doin' My Time." I believe that was the first record. I have it on the Red Barn label. Another one was "Will You Be Satisfied That Way." I was to get the only records they pressed up. But later on they started to distribute these records.

A man called me from Knoxville, Tennessee, and he said, "We'd like you to come down here and work with some of our boys." And I said, "You must be putting me on," 'cause I'd never been to Knoxville in my life, hardly heard of it. And he said, "Did you write a song called 'Will You Be Satisfied That Way'?" And I said, "Yes." "And do you have it on Red Barn Records?" And I said, "Yes, but you don't have any of them down there." And he said, "Well, I think you'd better come down here and see, 'cause it's the number-one record here in Knoxville."

I did go to Knoxville and it was, it was number one! I was wined and dined and treated like a king, and I didn't know how to take all that. People like Carl Smith, the Sauceman Brothers, Carl Butler and Pearl, everybody. They were there on the station, but I was the only one *making* records. *Big deal!* Red Barn Records at that *(laughs)*.

I had tried to get with companies before I made my Red Barn record. I had sent the same songs I recorded at Red Barn to [the] three or four labels [we had back then]. They either didn't send them back or they wrote back and told me they couldn't use me. I had sent the same song. But after this song hit so big in Knoxville . . . then I had the opportunity to record with Capitol or anybody I wanted to go with. That is really where it started.

"Doin' My Time," I was fortunate that that has become a classic in the bluegrass field as well as the country field. I wrote "Say Goodbye Like You Say Hello." It was a hit song for Ernest Tubb; he was really hot at that time and I sent the song to him. Then I had a song called "I Found My Girl in the U.S.A.," which got the BMI award. "Don't Give Your Heart to a Rambler," "Will You Be Satisfied That Way." Quite a few songs. "You Don't Know My Mind." That also has become a standard. I'm very proud of it. And I'm extremely proud of the fact that other people [do my songs].

WRITING SONGS

I never sit down and write any words unless I have a melody that goes on with it. Usually the words and melody come together. And usually the title comes into my mind first. If it sounds like a good title, I'll try to go from there. Something that I can repeat over and over at the end of the verses. I follow through with that, but I might write a song down and go back and change it many, many times. You can always go back and rearrange it, change the melody and the words till you get it down to where you think it ought to be. I believe in having a song to a point where no one needs to take the song and change it. That's a pet peeve of mine for someone to take a song of mine and rewrite it. I feel like I've spent enough time on it myself—although people don't *do* the songs the same way; I don't mind that—but when they take your song and tear it all up, if they're going to do that, they ought to write the songs themselves.

What inspires my songs? It's all life. It's the way that I know people live, the way I've lived myself. To me that is the song of life.

They're not all good songs [but] I have songs by the hundreds on paper and I have an awful lot of tapes. *(Betty yells from the kitchen where she has been busy washing dishes, "There are an awful lot of good songs, too! A lot nobody has even heard yet!")* All my songs aren't on tape yet. I write 'em and some of them are good and some of them are not.

Some people say they write when they are down and out; I can't. If I'm real down and out, I can't write my kind of song at all. If I'm in a happy-go-lucky frame of mind, I can write bluegrass songs. Well, I just can't concentrate on anything when I'm down.

"Take Me Home in a Song," I wrote it for just the way I felt at a festival. "Take Me Home," kinda dedicated to the festivalgoers.

(I asked Jimmie about influences other than Jimmie Rodgers.) Bill Monroe had talked to me at so many different times, and he'd tell me, "Jimmie, you should work a show for me." And occasionally I'd go to Bean Blossom and work a show for Bill Monroe. And he would always say these things to me and I thought, "Well, I don't know if I can do bluegrass or not." But I loved bluegrass 'cause I'd heard Bill and Charlie Monroe, the Monroe Brothers; they were people I dearly admired from hearing them on the radio before I ever met Bill Monroe. And finally I decided after I moved here to Nashville and I talked with him again, I decided that if he thought I could do that, then I ought to try it. He believed in me. And Bill Monroe was *the* man, the originator of the bluegrass music. And I found that it wasn't hard for me to do at all after I went out. I was lucky to have songs that had been accepted in the bluegrass field before I went out there. It wasn't like somebody going on stage and the people not knowing the songs. When I went out there to do "Doin' My Time," "You Don't Know My Mind," things like that, they knew 'em and they loved 'em.

And now when I go out, they don't bother with my songs too much. I'm proud when they do, but sometimes it sort of gets you when a couple of acts go out, and knowing you're there, they go out and do your songs first. I would rather they do them anyway. But I'm proud they do 'em.

LIFE BEYOND MUSIC

I am definitely not a twenty-four-hour-a-day music man. I'm really not. I love to write songs. I love to play music. There's a lot of times I don't want to play music or even hear music. This may sound strange out of a person who has made their livelihood out of the entertainment field. But this is true with me. I like to read, I like to watch some television. I love to get out more than anything in the world and go to fish. Just get out in the country where I can just walk through the woods and fields and picnic or just things like that. I love the country. That's my hobbies; mostly it's things like that.

I'm married. My wife's name is Betty and we have one boy, Jimmie, and he's twenty-two years old. Now Betty plays a pretty good guitar and sings and we used to sing some together. She helps me on quite a few of my songs now. My boy sings when you can get him to sing. I've got a tape of him doing "You Don't Know My Mind," and if you wouldn't know, you would think it's me! But I can't get him into the field. He works up in Cincinnati in a record-pressing plant where they press my records.

LOOKING BACK AND AHEAD

One of the big days, I guess, I've loved a lot was going back home to Berea. *(Jimmie was from the community of Blue Lick, just outside Berea.)* They made it my day down there. We had an annual thing down there, every year, me and Red Foley. [He's] from there, too. We'd go back for the Lion's Club and do this show free and they'd give the money to whatever they wanted to. So we all had a day down there. Bradley [Kincaid] had a day, Red Foley had a day. And then I had a day. That was a big honor to me. A parade in your honor and they give you the key to the city.

I still go back to Berea at least once a year. I'll go maybe to the hardware store or a restaurant, places that the kids I went to school with [might be], I go in and see them all.

I'm happy with where I'm at today in music. I realize that if I had started today there's a lot more money in it now than when we worked back years ago. Of course, Bill Monroe and everybody else can tell you about that; the times wasn't that good and you didn't make as much money. I'm still happy with what I'm doing. I still write. I love to write. I don't know how many more years I'll be active playing festivals and things like that. But right at the present time, I have no idea of retiring. And I'll continue to write and I'm still very deeply involved in what I love more than anything in the world, my music.

I will be doing an album of some new songs and going back and getting some of the old ones that [I have] the master tapes on and reissue those. But I will have some new things. I'll continue to write and play songs as I can with other artists. That is a *great* thrill for someone else to record a song.

I sometimes feel that maybe that other song is out there that I can still write that'll be bigger than "Doin' My Time" or something. But I'm happy that I had those. They've really kept my spirits alive. Every time I look in the *Bluegrass Unlimited* or *Pickin'* magazine, where they review albums, and I'll look to see what they've recorded, and when I find "You Don't Know My Mind" or "Don't Give Your Heart to a Rounder" by Tony Rice or somebody, I'm really happy.

I would like to do an album some time of my heroes in bluegrass and country, their songs. I had that opportunity one time and didn't do it. In bluegrass, it would have been Bill Monroe, in country Roy Acuff and Ernest Tubb, Jimmie Rodgers, Hank Williams.

—JIMMIE SKINNER / 1909–1979

Irish button accordionist Joe Burke.
Tommy Makem's Irish Pavilion, New
York City, January 31, 1986.

Above: Chris Parkinson of the House Band from Ireland. Philadelphia Folk Festival, Schwenksville, Pennsylvania, August 26, 1989.

Right: Patrick Sauber, who plays banjo, guitar, mandolin and accordion for Skip Gorman and the Waddie Pals, proponents of cowboy music. He recently appeared in the folk music spoof *A Mighty Wind*. Roots and Branches Stage, Bluegrass Fan Fest, Galt House, Louisville, Kentucky, October 19, 2002.

Above: Veteran bluegrass singer-songwriter-guitarist John Herald jams with legendary guitarist Doc Watson. Waterloo Folk Festival, Waterloo Village, Stanhope, New Jersey, September 3, 1984.

Right: "Classic" Country Gentleman Eddie Adcock and Martha Adcock showcase in a hospitality suite. World of Bluegrass, Galt House, Louisville, Kentucky, October 2002.

Arlo Guthrie. Philadelphia Folk Festival, Schwenksville, Pennsylvania, August 25, 2001.

Left: Dobro player Gene Wooten with Country Gazette. In the foreground on banjo is Alan Munde; Roland White is obscured on mandolin. Lone Star Café, New York City, May 22, 1988.

Above: Cindy Cashdollar, sitting in with Gone At Last from Norway. Cashdollar toured for many years as pedal steel player for Asleep At The Wheel and now leads her own western swing band. Lone Star Café, New York City, August 29, 1986.

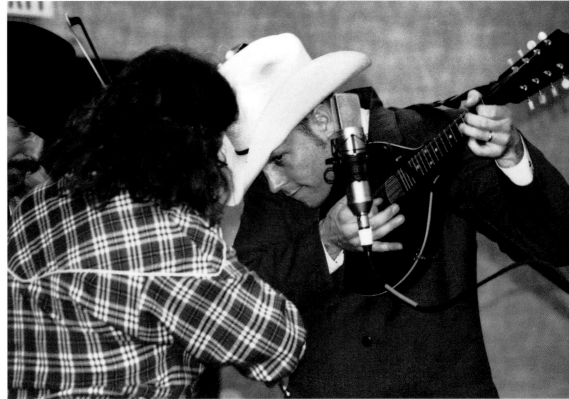

Above: The Wilders from Kansas City, Missouri.
Mandolinist Phil Wade challenges Betse Ellis's fid-
dle playing. The Wilders describe their music as
"old-time country tunes from the golden age."
Roots and Branches Stage, Bluegrass Fan Fest,
Galt House, Louisville, Kentucky, October 19, 2002.

Left: Dave Markowitz with Dan Weiss looking on
(Wretched Refuse String Band). The Bottom Line,
New York City, January 20, 1991.

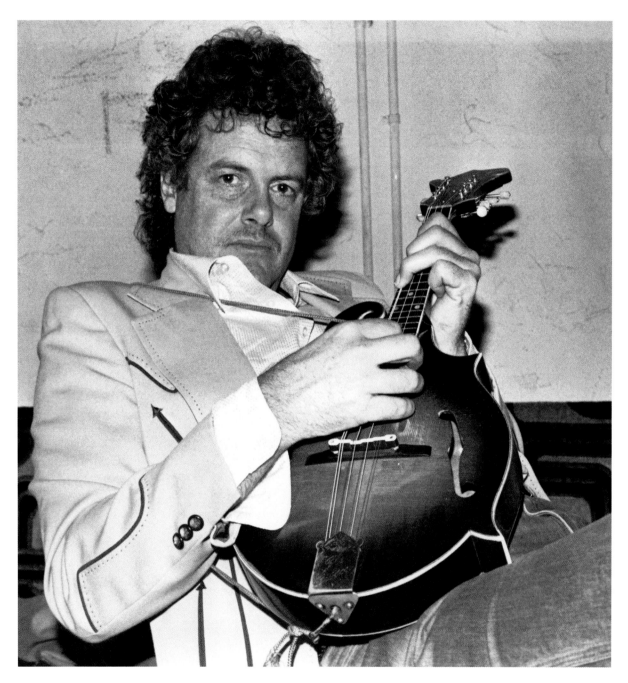

Peter Rowan. We were chatting back-stage in the dressing room. Peter was picking casually while we talked and when he looked up, I snapped the unposed shot. I had a short-range wide angle lens on my camera which gave the photo an interesting per-spective. Lone Star Café, New York City, March 27, 1985.

Above: Josh White, Jr. Old Songs Festival of Traditional Music and Dance. Fairgrounds, Altamont, New York, June 26, 1999.

Left: Country star Keith Whitley. Lone Star Café, New York City, May 28, 1987.

★ ★ ★

VASSAR CLEMENTS
FIDDLES HILLBILLY JAZZ

One of the most versatile fiddlers, Vassar Clements is like no other. Dubbed the "Hillbilly Jazz Fiddler," he has toured and recorded with artists as diverse as Stephane Grappelli, the Grateful Dead, John Hartford, the Allman Brothers, Peter Rowan, Northern Lights, Nitty Gritty Dirt Band, and David Grisman, to name but a few. He appeared on the groundbreaking album *Will the Circle Be Unbroken*, as well as on the two subsequent volumes.

At the time of this interview, he had just released *Hillbilly Jazz Rides Again*. Here is a glimpse into the man, the musician. Recorded February 3, 1987, New York City.

SL: *What makes Vassar Clements tick musically?*
VC: Music. That's about it.

SL: *Any kind of music?*
VC: Yeah, if it's good.

SL: *Where do you draw your innovations from? Who were your inspirations?*
VC: I think big bands. Glenn Miller. I grew up in the big band era. I just love rhythm, you know. So partially the big bands, partially it was just born in me, I guess.

SL: *Can you describe your style?*
VC: No, I don't know. How do you describe something like that? It's all from feeling. I don't have any earthly idea what's going to happen. I know maybe the beginning and the end, but in between I don't know.

SL: *Have you ever tried to imitate anybody's style?*
VC: Yes, when I first started, Chubby Wise. He was my idol. He played with Bill Monroe, '47, I believe. Still, to this day, he has the prettiest notes I ever heard.

SL: *How old were you when you picked up the fiddle? Was it your first and only instrument?*
VC: I kind of picked up the guitar first, maybe a couple or three months before I did the fiddle. I was seven, I think.

SL: *Are you completely self-taught?*
VC: Oh, yeah.

SL: *No formal training?*
VC: No. I didn't even know how to hold it *(laughs)*.

SL: *Is music your life?*
VC: Oh, yeah.

SL: *And if not music, what would you be doing?*
VC: Oh, I don't have any earthly idea.

SL: *Did you ever set career goals for yourself?*
VC: No, not really. I didn't know anything except I wanted to play.

SL: *How hard and long did you practice fiddle as a kid?*
VC: I know it was quite a bit. I'd get disgusted and almost want to cry. Then five minutes later I'd go pick it up again. You just keep learning enough to keep you rollin' on. And I'm sure I practiced a lot. 'Cause I would practice just trying to move the bow. I didn't even know! I knew that I wanted to move it without scratching, while going back and forth. Then I had to figure out how to put my fingers in between it to make it work. I guess that's the reason you call it "my style" or something. Because I depend on the rhythm. I don't play the rhythm like most of the players do.

SL: *Do you practice now?*
VC: Sometimes! *(Laughs.)* Every once in a while when I get a chance.

SL: *In recent years, you've been handling more lead vocal work. Do you enjoy being up front in the spotlight doing that?*
VC: I hate it! No, I don't enjoy the spotlight. I really don't. It unnerves me. I want to play. I'll get used to it maybe, but it's going to take a little while. 'Cause I'm having to remember words while I'm playing and everything. I've just got to learn how to do it all the time *(laughs)*.

SL: *Are you by nature shy?*
VC: Yeah, I guess so. Well, I'm not shy necessarily when I'm playing. But I don't care too much about talking. I don't have a whole lot to say [to the audience], except I'm glad they're there, you know, and hope they love the music. I don't know any jokes to tell people. I'm thinking about music anyway and wanting them to like it.

SL: *Where are you more comfortable, in a recording studio or on stage?*

VC: Not a recording studio. I would hate to stay in there all the time. After about six hours or seven hours of that, I've got to get out.

SL: *In all the genres your music touches upon—bluegrass, jazz, blues, swing, country, and others—where does your heart lie?*
VC: Rhythm swing.

SL: *Has bluegrass become more refined and more acceptable to a wider audience in recent years?*
VC: I would say yes, because a few years ago, I could have gone out there with five horns and things, and man, it's not that bluegrass. See what I'm talking about? You have to really *know* what bluegrass is. But it's good in a way, because it's getting spread more. Whether it's bluegrass or not, who cares.

SL: *Can we really define bluegrass?*
VC: I hope they can't. Because if you do, then you've got that little circle right there and that's all. It's really the feeling. I don't see why you got to use upright bass, I don't see why you can't use electric.

SL: *Why do you think your fiddle playing appeals to a wide variety of people who are usually purists in what they listen to, bluegrass enthusiasts, jazz enthusiasts, country, etc.?*
VC: Well, I've asked some people that I got to know real good, you know, because you don't really see it yourself. Every one of them said it was the feeling. So there's got to be something to that.

SL: *What do you have your sights set on for the future?*
VC: All I want to do is play music, and survive playing music enough to make a living playing music. The main thing is people liking it. Because if they don't like it, what's the use of playing? I'm playing for myself but I'm playing also because I want them to like it. And if they don't like it, that really hurts. So my goal is to just keep learning, just keep playing, you know.

SL: *How would you like to be remembered in the music history books?*
VC: Just remembered! *(Laughs.)*

Bill Keith (banjo), Roy Huskey (bass, obscured), Vassar Clements (fiddle), Peter Rowan (guitar), Marty Stuart (mandolin). Lone Star Café, New York City, July 26, 1984.

Dueling boxes? (Left) French-Canadian group Barachois' Chuck Arsenault on tuba with Albert Arsenault playing vegetable steamer while using a box for brushed percussion. (Above) Martin Parker, percussionist with the Patty Loveless Band, prefers an overnight delivery service box. Delaware Valley Bluegrass Festival, Woodstown, New Jersey, August 29, 2003, and August 31, 2002, respectively.

Father and son. Left: Doc Watson checking out a fellow musician's banjo in a dressing room backstage. Delaware Valley Bluegrass Festival, Woodstown, New Jersey, September 1, 2001. Above: Merle Watson. Waterloo Folk Festival, Waterloo Village, Stanhope, New Jersey, September 3, 1984.

★ ★ ★

DOC WATSON

"APPLAUSE IS LIKE AN AMPLIFIED FRIENDLY HANDSHAKE"

Random thoughts, excerpted from an interview with Doc Watson.
John Harms Center for the Performing Arts (now Bergen
Performing Arts Center), Englewood, New Jersey, November 7, 2002.

"Somehow, when I go on the stage knowing that fans are out there to hear me, the music is fresh all over again. It's like tasting something that you've really enjoyed eating, but you hadn't had that particular goody, we'll say, in three or four years. And it works the same way. If I play good music, the best I can do here tonight, and I go down yonder just tomorrow night, a good audience welcomes me on the stage, it'll be just as fresh for me to play then. Unless I'm really bothered by something that preempts the warmth and the interest in the music. The applause is like an amplified friendly handshake, however many people's out there, and that sparks the interest all over again."

"One of the things that thrilled me was the very beginning when Merle first went on the stage with me at Stern Grove Park at Berkeley Folk Festival. Oh, I was just proud as I could be. He played back-up guitar to everything I played on that festival and didn't miss a chord. And when we came off the stage, I said, 'Son, how'd you feel out there?' He says, 'I wanted to run.'"

"Merle and I did two albums. One was *Southbound*. It wasn't live. It was in the studio in New York City for Vanguard. And the other one was *Doc and Merle On Stage*. One of the shows was Town Hall in New York and the other one was up in Ithaca, Cornell University. The spontaneity of the show, the way it sounds on the album . . . I ad-libbed the talk, the narrative between the songs without thinking about it. It just happened. The shows were just as smooth as they could be. And those two [shows], they made an album from. And when that album got out there, we got more comments on that. I had done several albums for Vanguard before that, including the *Southbound* album, but it seemed to me after that album, *Doc and Merle On Stage,* interest in our music began to grow. I think that was the turning point in my career."

Above: Bill Monroe and his Blue Grass Boys, photographed from the balcony directly above them at the Lone Star Café, New York City, March 17, 1987.

Right: Considered by many the spokesperson for bluegrass since Monroe's passing, Ricky Skaggs trades mandolin chops with eleven-year-old Sierra Hull. Bluegrass Fan Fest, Louisville, Kentucky, October 18, 2002.

Piedmont blues stylists "Bowling Green" John Cephas, guitar, and Phil Wiggins, harmonica, join Doc Watson on stage, along with fiddler Mark O'Connor. Merle Watson Memorial Festival (now MerleFest), Wilkesboro, North Carolina, May 1, 1993.

Left: Del McCoury Band's Ronnie McCoury. Delaware Valley Bluegrass Festival, Woodstown, New Jersey, August 30, 2002.

Above: Jesse McReynolds. Alexander Hall's Richardson Auditorium dressing room, Princeton University, Princeton, New Jersey, October 10, 1981.

Above: Irish Uilleann pipes master Jerry O'Sullivan.
Right: Eileen Ivers fires up her fiddle to challenge
O'Sullivan's pipes. Philadelphia Folk Festival,
Schwenksville, Pennsylvania, August 25, 2001.

Above: The Osborne Brothers, Sonny (banjo) and Bobby (mandolin), joined by legendary bluegrass singer Mac Wiseman (guitar). In the shadows are Terry Eldredge (guitar) and Gene Wooten (dobro). Delaware Valley Bluegrass Festival, Woodstown, New Jersey, September 5, 1992.

Left: James Reams and the Barnstormers (left to right), Mickey Maguire, Mark Farrell, James Reams, and Carl Hayano. World of Bluegrass, Galt House, Louisville, Kentucky, October 2002.

Mike Seeger playing jaw harp.
It was an intimate auditorium and I
really did not want to keep snapping
photos, because every shutter click
resonated. I had to wait to shoot only
during the loudest moments in the
music. Somehow I knew when I took
this frame that this was that one shot
any photographer hopes for per roll
of film, the one that makes it worth
the effort to expend a roll. Traditional
Music Festival, Grand Opera House,
Wilmington, Delaware, June 9, 2001.

Above: Cherryholmes, a family bluegrass band. From left, B. J. on fiddle, Sandy Lee (Mom) on mandolin, Molly Kate on fiddle, Jere (Pop) on bass, Cia Leigh on banjo, Skip with guitar. Warming up in the green room at Bluegrass Fan Fest, Galt House, Louisville, Kentucky, October 2002.

Left: Squares and contra dances were called on the Market Street Mall by Pete LaBerge (not shown), while a pickup band provided the music. Musicians pictured are Clare Milliner playing fiddle, Woody Woodring on guitar, Bob Taylor playing bass, and Frank Scott on banjo. Traditional Music Festival, in front of the Grand Opera House, Wilmington, Delaware, June 9, 2001.

★ ★ ★
"TASTE THE TRADITIONAL" WITH THE BLUEGRASS BAND

The Bluegrass Band was a short-lived ensemble whose goal was to present lively, homegrown music in which listeners could "taste the traditional," as its publicity catchphrase touted. Founded January 1, 1982, the group comprised topflight musicians and entertainers who offered a showcase of music mixed with light country humor. Each band member came with a solid set of credentials. However, by the end of the next year, the group had dissolved, the individuals going on to make their own way in other groups and realms of the music.

Most notable was the subsequent formation in 1984 of the Nashville Bluegrass Band, whose banjo player, Alan O'Bryant, had been guitarist and lead vocalist for The Bluegrass Band. The Nashville Bluegrass Band has been in the spotlight in recent years with its involvement in the Down from the Mountain and Great High Mountain tours, focusing on the music from the films *O Brother, Where Art Thou?*, *Down from the Mountain*, and *Cold Mountain*.

The founder of The Bluegrass Band was Butch Robins. Robins is an exceptional banjo player whose long list of credits includes spots with Bill Monroe and the Blue Grass Boys, New Grass Revival, and Wilma Lee and Stoney Cooper.

O'Bryant had played banjo for James Monroe and the Midnight Ramblers and for the Front Porch String Band, and he had filled in for two weeks as a Blue Grass Boy. He switched to guitar for The Bluegrass Band.

Fiddle player Blaine Sprouse started out professionally with Jimmy Martin and the Sunny Mountain Boys, and went on to James Monroe's group and then to Charlie Louvin's band and Jim and Jesse and the Virginia Boys. Considered a Kenny Baker protégé, he left The Bluegrass Band after only a few months to become a sideman with the Osborne Brothers.

David Sebring's background includes touring or recording with such artists as Uncle Walt's Band, Norman Blake, Buck White, and Hazel Dickens. Also a guitarist with a penchant for early jazz, he played bass for the group.

Ed Dye played dobro and bones in the band and added much colorful humor to the group's performances. Previously a television producer-director, he gigged with a variety of Nashville-area bands, including the Shinbone Alley All-Stars, before joining up with The Bluegrass Band.

In the final analysis, while not long for this world as a group, The Bluegrass Band likely helped set in motion a higher awareness that traditional music could be taken to a broader audience successfully and with great entertainment value. Talent, an attitude to get it out there, and the publicity smarts to do so were all part of the package The Bluegrass Band set out to assemble.

Here are choice excerpts from a two-session interview with The Bluegrass Band, which never saw print because they disbanded so quickly. Conducted August 7, 1982, Tarrytown, New York, and September 10, 1982, East Windsor, New Jersey.

SL: *How and why did this band evolve?*
ALAN: It's the brainchild of Butch Robins.
BUTCH: We'd all picked with each other at various times during our career and heard the sounds we made together. It just seems like the talent somehow merged through that. It's a contrived effort to try to put together a band that could play legitimate bluegrass music, the full range of the music . . . and do it in the context of an entertainment show. And these are just *the best* musicians that I know.
ED: And we are very open to presenting it as best we can.
BUTCH: We have developed a format here where any one of five talents has [the opportunity to] expand on himself completely, whether it be Ed as an entertainer and musician, or me as a banjo player and musician, or Blaine as a fiddle player and musician, or David as a bass player and musician . . .

SL: *You've said you don't feel you are innovators—yet. Do you want to be?*
BUTCH: Innovators in the sense of writing our own tunes and writing our own songs, that's part of our expression. But we don't want to alienate a grassroots bluegrass audience by bringing everything out new. We would like to make them our friends and fans, too, as well as introduce this to the areas of the entertainment world where bluegrass is a respectable word yet no act

has ever been able to get through those doors. We're trying to keep it alive.

SL: *What is the long-range goal of The Bluegrass Band?*
BUTCH: We want to be in a position to play the music in a way that it pays for itself. We're professional musicians. The dollars are on our minds. It's very difficult to make any kind of music pay for itself to keep it on the road. We would like to be able to play this music as much as we can, in its pure form, and have it support the traveling road band as a show.
ALAN: The success of a band, this band I think, at the end of the first year, is not measured in how much money it made but in how well, at the end of that time, it's able to *attract* dollars.
BUTCH: One of the premises behind us is we're working toward an ideal of only being in this band four to six months out of the year. And the other time is meant for everybody to pursue their own particular musical tastes, musical projects. And the band is geared to that. This is a show band we put together. We assembled the best talent we can get and tried to put together a show to make dollars. The rest of it is everybody's own thing.

Above all, we've got to keep the guys interested in music and interested in the music of our band, but most of all interested in music. It's awful easy to burn out on music.

SL: *You don't just pick and sing when you are on stage; you convey a well-rounded show. How hard do you work at stage presence?*
ED: We've got to entertain the folks. If you've got a stage show, you have to entertain them. Segovia does

that, if you've ever seen him work. He knows exactly what he's doing. He may not do some of the Henny Youngman jokes, but he'll stop his show for latecomers. Or if anybody's coughing or raising hell, he'll stop playing. But he does it in such a way he keeps attention on the stage, on all his movement and gestures. He is a showman. The showmanship that he employs is, of course, his musicianship, his mastery of his ax. He knows these little tricks to present his music so well. And in the end, the people are entertained. Ravi Shankar is another master showman.

Ed Dye aptly summed up the music and musicianship of The Bluegrass Band. "Our objective has been [to] bring what we're doing to life with honesty."

Above: The Bluegrass Band finds an unlikely audience at the grand opening of a brand-new shopping mall. In view, fiddler Blaine Sprouse, bass player David Sebring, with the group's founder, Butch Robins, obscured up front on banjo. Quakerbridge Mall, Lawrenceville, New Jersey, February 13, 1982.

Right: The Bluegrass Band. Left to right: Ed Dye, David Sebring, Alan O'Bryant, Butch Robins. Beyond the shot is Blaine Sprouse. Grand Old Country Music Show, Lyndhurst, Tarrytown, New York, August 7, 1982.

Above: Nashville Bluegrass Band. Left to right: Roland White, Pat Enright, Gene Libbea, Alan O'Bryant, Stuart Duncan. Left: Alan O'Bryant lifts up his banjo to make his vocals "shine" or reflect off the banjo head into the microphone for projection and effect. Winterhawk (now Grey Fox) Bluegrass Festival, Ancramdale, New York, July 22, 1989.

INDEX TO PHOTOS